TAROT CARD
COMPANION

MASTER THE ART OF TAROT READING

VICTORIA MAXWELL

To all the tarot readers of the past who have paved the way for us here and now, and to all The Fools starting out on their tarot journey.

A Rockpool book

PO Box 252
Summer Hill
NSW 2130
Australia

rockpoolpublishing.com
Follow us! f ⓘ rockpoolpublishing
Tag your images with #rockpoolpublishing

ISBN: 9781923208094
Published in 2025 by Rockpool Publishing

Copyright text © Victoria Maxwell 2025
Copyright design & photos © Rockpool Publishing 2025

All rights reserved. No part of this publication may be reproduced, stored in a retrieval system, or transmitted in any form or by any means, electronic, mechanical, photocopying, recording or otherwise, without the prior written permission of the publisher.

Design and typesetting by Christine Armstrong, Rockpool Publishing
Edited by Lisa Macken
Photos by Claire Eastman Photography
claireeastmanphotography.com.au

 A catalogue record for this book is available from the National Library of Australia

Printed and bound in China
10 9 8 7 6 5 4 3 2 1

CONTENTS

INTRODUCTION	1
HOW TO USE THIS BOOK	7
A BRIEF HISTORY OF THE TAROT	11
Chapter 1 INTRODUCTION TO THE TAROT SYSTEM	15
Chapter 2 TAROT READING BASICS	35
Chapter 3 NEXT STEPS	49
Chapter 4 ADVANCING YOUR READINGS	65
Chapter 5 TAROT SPREADS	89
Chapter 6 EXPANDED CARD MEANINGS	131
Chapter 7 TROUBLESHOOTING GUIDE	295
ABOUT THE AUTHOR	300

INTRODUCTION

Are you ready to awaken your intuition, step into your power and create a heart-led life filled with magic? Imagine understanding your soul's purpose with clarity, moving through life with more confidence and self-trust and having access to ancient occult secrets that have guided mystics for centuries. If that lights you up then welcome, gorgeous soul: this book is your guide to all of that and more!

It might seem like a tall order for 78 little cards, but tarot is so much more than just a deck. It's your direct line to inner wisdom, a mirror for your soul and a tool for tapping into profound guidance that can help you make empowered choices and manifest incredible things in your life.

I experienced my first tarot reading in the early 2000s in Sydney, Australia. At the end of a night out me and my friends stumbled out of the pub to head home, but I stopped short when I saw a man sitting on a milk crate on a corner, a deck of tarot cards on a makeshift table in front of him. In that moment I just *knew* I had to get a reading. My friends tried to stop me, calling it hocus pocus and a waste of money. Thankfully I ignored them and took a seat on the milk crate.

While I don't remember everything from that reading there were a few things that still stick with me, especially The Star card. The reader told me that the little bird in that card would always guide me, and he talked about doors closing and things being finished. I knew immediately it was about a relationship I had to end and I did so shortly after that reading, and it was indeed for my highest good! It wasn't until years later that I discovered the bird on The Star card is a symbol of the ancient Egyptian god Thoth, who is now one of my most cherished guides.

I always kept a look out on that corner, but I never saw that reader again. Sometimes I wonder if he was a spirit guide or angel, or even Thoth popping down to get me on my path. Whoever he was, I am so thankful I found him and for the guidance and wisdom he shared, which has stayed with me through every step of my journey.

Soon after that reading I bought my first tarot deck from a metaphysical shop in Newtown. After weeks of agonising over which of about three decks to choose from I eventually got home with my Hanson-Roberts tarot, knowing deep within my soul that this was it for me. This little deck of cards was going to tell me everything I needed to know and show me how wonderful my future would be but, alas: those first few weeks, months and *years* of trying to read the tarot were painful, slow and confusing. I knew that deck contained important secrets, but I didn't understand what the heck all those old timey–looking people riding horses had to do with my life. Still, I persisted and I carried that deck with me all over the world, pulling it out in times of need.

In 2011 I was given a cosmic nudge to get serious about my spiritual journey after years of dabbling. I dusted off my deck: it was time to get to grips with the tarot, and this time all the mystical pennies dropped. I had an incredible experience one afternoon in which I felt as though I was not learning the tarot but *remembering* how to read the cards. In just a few hours I went from relying on the book for meanings to doing full spreads for myself and understanding *exactly* what the guidance meant.

✦ Once you start on your tarot adventure you will never stop learning. Twenty something years later I am still learning something new about the tarot each time I look at the cards.

Tarot has changed my life in so many ways for the better. Whenever I feel unsure or unsteady, am dealing with difficulties or times of change or when I feel good and want to manifest more magic in my life, the tarot is always there to guide me. It is my most heart-felt intention that this book serves as a guiding star for you on your tarot journey, lighting the path to your most magical, empowered life.

May your inner knowledge and connection with the highest wisdom be activated, may all fears be dissolved and may your tarot readings always be clear and empowering.

And so it is!

With so much love,

Vix x

HOW TO USE THIS BOOK

You can use this book with any tarot deck you have, but you will find it most useful with a Rider-Waite-Smith (RWS) style deck. Most tarot decks are based on this system even if they have some variations. If your deck has 22 major cards, 56 minor cards with illustrations for the four suits of Wands, Cups, Swords and Pentacles and the court cards of Page, Knight, Queen and King, you most likely have a RWS-style deck.

If you are brand new to tarot, start at the beginning and work your way through. Pay particular attention to the sections on how to prepare your energy for a reading and how to know who you're communicating with through your readings. Read the advice about scary cards and predictions so you can empower yourself from the outset. You can also read through the expanded card meanings chapter from front to back, which will give you a good grounding in understanding the symbolism and messages of the cards.

If you already have some experience with tarot this book can help you gain more confidence in your readings and develop your intuition further. Take what you need from the basics and next steps sections, then head to the advanced practices to help you go deeper into the mysteries and magic of tarot. No matter where you are on your journey, feel free to flip around and trust your intuition to help you find what you're looking for.

You do not need to know everything before you start reading for yourself. There's a plethora of tarot spreads included in this book for every situation, so grab your deck, prepare your energy and start reading for yourself right now!

If you follow all the advice in this book but still struggle to make sense of your readings, head to the Troubleshooting section at the back of this book for advice on how to make sense of things.

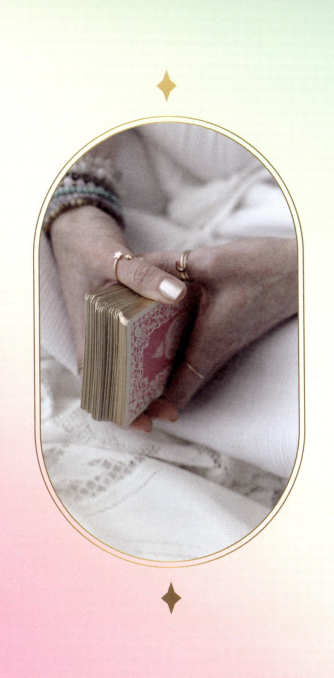

A BRIEF HISTORY OF THE TAROT

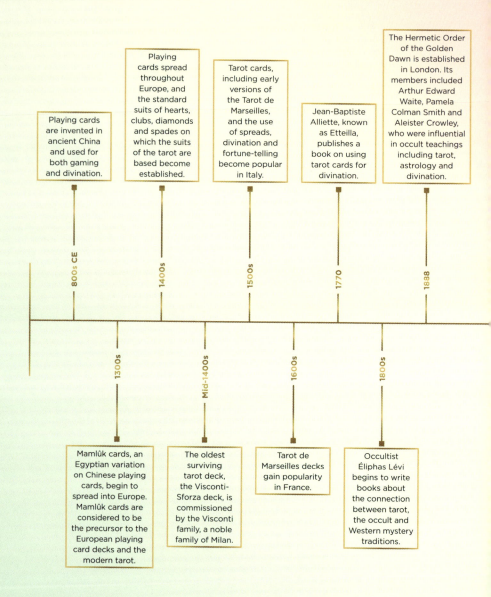

TAROT CARD COMPANION

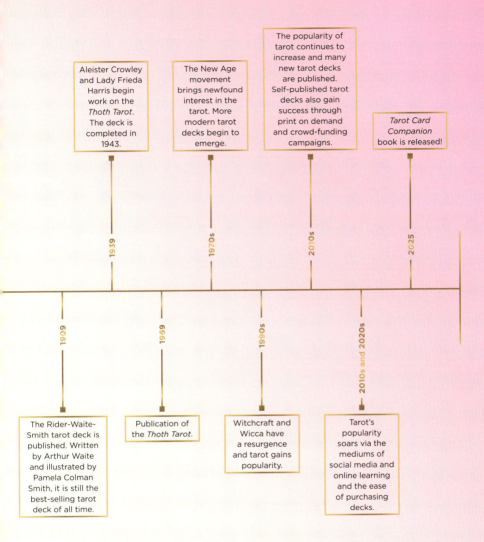

A brief history of the tarot

13

INTRODUCTION TO THE TAROT SYSTEM

A deck of tarot cards contains two types of cards: the major arcana and the minor arcana. 'Arcana' means 'secrets' or 'mysteries'.

The **major arcana** cards are the 22 tarot cards that are usually most recognisable such as The Magician, The Moon, The Lovers, The Devil and so on. Some tarot decks include only these 22 cards, and they can be taken out of a 78-card deck and used in a reading just on their own.

The major arcana cards often represent the bigger or *major* aspects of life and take you on what's known as The Fool's journey, from The Fool's first step off the cliff through all the adventures along the way until reaching fulfilment of worldly success depicted in The World card. Each card in the major arcana mirrors the most impactful experiences in life, especially on the journey of personal growth, spiritual discovery and soul expansion.

The 56 cards of the **minor arcana** reflect the more everyday aspects of life. Similar to a deck of playing cards split into four suits, each suit in the tarot relates to an element: Wands to fire, Cups to water, Swords to air and Pentacles to earth. You may see alterations to the names of suits in different decks – for example, pentacles as coins or wands as rods – but they have the same elemental energies.

Take out The Lovers from the major arcana and the Two of Cups from the minor arcana from your deck and notice the differences. These cards can both mean love in readings, but their energy is quite different. The Two of Cups is a strong connection with a friend, co-worker, collaborator or someone you've just started dating, while The Lovers card depicts a much more intense bond, a soul-mate relationship or deeper love of the self and connection with the divine. That's the difference between the major and minor arcana.

Within the minor arcana are 16 **court cards** in a deck, four in each suit. In the RWS system the court cards are Pages, Knights, Queens and Kings. Pages are youthful, Knights are adventurous, Queens are intuitive leaders and Kings project experience and success. The court cards are the personalities of the tarot. They can represent people in your life but they also show up as aspects of yourself, energies that would be useful to embody, and sometimes they point to things within you that require a little work.

The energies and archetypes of the 16 court cards are within us all. We all have masculine and feminine aspects, we can all be watery, fiery, grounded and airy at times and we're all capable of expressing youthful enthusiasm or deep wisdom beyond our years.

A note on gender roles: many traditional or older tarot decks depict the court cards in traditional gender roles. A good way to think of the court cards in modern times is to focus more on the elemental correspondences and general energy and traits of the court cards over gender. It is also a common concern by some that the Kings come after the Queens as though they are higher in rank. They are equal in power but have different traits. You can think of them both as monarchs, and if you like you can order your court cards Page, Knight, King, Queen.

Tarot time!

Go through your deck and put your cards into order, checking the meanings section in this book for the order if needed, so you can see how the system works. Consider the differences you notice in the imagery, energy or feeling between the majors, minors and court cards. Think about or journal on the following:

✦ Which cards are you most drawn to: the majors, minors or the court cards?
✦ Which major card are you most drawn to right now, and why do you think that is?
✦ Which minor card is speaking to you, and what is it saying?
✦ Which court card do you feel an affinity with, and why does it resonate with you?

PREPARING FOR READINGS

In the following pages you'll learn everything you need to know about how to prepare for readings, from choosing your first tarot deck to communicating with your guides and grounding, clearing and protecting your energy.

Choosing a tarot deck

There are many myths around how a tarot deck should come into your life, and one of the most common is that your tarot deck must be gifted to you. No one knows where this myth came from: it may have been a way to protect the occult secrets of the tarot, or perhaps it was the only way you could get your hands on a deck back then. However, times have changed and there is now access to many incredible metaphysical stores and websites, so you don't need to adhere to centuries-old myths with no relevance to modern times.

Over the years I have both bought and been gifted many decks. I do feel a special connection with decks that have been gifted to me by someone important to me or decks I've bought in a special place and time, but I've never noticed a difference in how effective they are in readings.

A quick search online or a visit to any metaphysical bookshop may leave you feeling overwhelmed at the options when it comes to choosing your first, second or hundredth tarot deck. There's the Tarot de Marseilles, Thoth tarot, RWS tarot, retro tarot decks from the 1970s and 1980s, modern-style decks, themed decks, decks based on your favourite television show: anything you're into has probably been made into a tarot deck!

While themed decks can be a lot of fun they are not always that easy to read with, even for advanced readers, so for your first deck you can't go past a simple version of the Rider-Waite-Smith deck. My recommendation for those at the very beginning of their journey is *Your First Tarot* deck. Combining the original imagery of the RWS deck with a modern pastel colouring, this deck includes simple keywords on each card to give you a kick-start on your journey.

Some people believe that a tarot deck will contain all the energy of the person who used it before and the readings it has done in the past, but if you cleanse, clear, activate and bond with a second-hand deck in the ways mentioned in this book there's no reason why a pre-loved deck can't work just as well for you as a brand new one.

Don't overthink it, and don't let decision paralysis stop you from getting started. It's a nice idea that your first deck will come into your life in some magical way, but it's okay if you just buy or use whatever deck is available. With so many options out there you're bound to find a deck you fall in love with, but sometimes you end up with one that just isn't for you. If you find you're not bonding with your deck or struggling to read with it put it aside and, if you can, work with a different deck and see if that works for you instead.

If a deck no longer feels right for you, you can always gift it to a friend or donate, sell or swap it; check Facebook groups for tarot deck swaps. You can also use the cards on an altar, for spells (more about that later), in art projects, as bookmarks or as little gifts in cards or letters. Just be sure not to send anyone The Devil, Death or The Tower card if you want to stay on good terms!

Clearing your tarot deck

When you get your deck home start with clearing it of any energy it's picked up in the printing and distribution process, from being in the store or warehouse or being used by anyone else.

Clearing your deck quickly between readings will help keep your readings clear. You may like to perform a deeper cleanse of your deck on a new or full moon, after some big readings, after someone else has touched your cards or any time you feel the messages are getting murky, sluggish or tired.

TO CLEAR YOUR TAROT DECK YOU CAN TRY ANY OF THE FOLLOWING METHODS:

- ✦ Hold the deck in your left hand and knock on it with the knuckles of your right hand one to three times to tap out any negativity and old energy.
- ✦ Tap the edge or edges of the deck on a table.
- ✦ Blow or breathe onto your deck, which is a quick way to cleanse but also bond the deck with your energy.
- ✦ Waft incense or ethically sourced sage or palo santo smoke around and through the cards.
- ✦ Place cleansing crystals such as clear quartz or selenite on your deck. Wash the clear quartz afterwards and cleanse the selenite with sound or smoke.
- ✦ Play singing bowls, bells or tingshas over the cards.

✦ Hold the deck in your left hand, place your right hand just above the deck and visualise white light or reiki healing energy clearing through your deck.

✦ Separate the cards and lay them on the floor or a large table, then gently squirt a light mist of aura spray over the cards. Be very careful when using this technique, as too much water can warp the cards.

✦ Sunlight works well for both clearing and charging. Make sure the area is dry and don't leave the cards for too long or the colours may fade.

✦ Rub a diluted essential oil of your choosing onto your hands. Any cleansing oil will work well; try sage, peppermint, rosemary or eucalyptus. Wait until the oil is slightly absorbed into your skin, then give your deck a shuffle. Be careful with this method as you don't want your deck to get oily.

✦ One of the best ways to clear your deck is just by shuffling the cards.

✦ Re-order the cards: putting the cards back into their original order is a great way to reset the energy of the deck.

Charging your tarot deck

Charging your deck keeps it topped up with good energy and ready for readings. You can try any of these methods:

✦ Place a crystal on top of the deck, either in or out of the box when you're not using it. Amethyst is a favourite of many card readers as it's a very clearing, grounding and intuitive stone. You may like to use smoky quartz for protection, selenite or angelite for angelic connection, or clear quartz as a general all-purpose stone.

✦ If you have an altar or sacred space, let your deck rest and charge there until you are ready to use it again.

✦ Charge your deck on a windowsill during a full moon.

✦ Blowing on your cards will both cleanse and charge their energy.

Activating your tarot deck

Once your deck is clear you may like to activate your cards and bond your energy with them. Here is a ritual you might like to try:

✦ Clear the deck by knocking it three times with your knuckles or gently knocking the edge of the deck on a table or flat surface.

✦ Hold the deck at your heart and take a deep breath.

✦ Visualise a golden white or pink light at your heart, filling the cards with the light from your heart.

✦ Say the following or a version of your own mentally or out loud: *'Thank you, cards, for coming into my life. Thank you for being a powerful tool for guidance, support, healing and transformation. Thank you for helping me to connect more deeply with my heart, intuition and higher self and my guides and angels and all beings from the highest realms of love, light, peace and truth who guide me. Thank you for guiding*

I began doing readings for family and friends and then for strangers on the internet, and soon I had many regular clients and I've been reading professionally ever since. I have learned so much about the tarot since the early 2000s, and I'm so excited to be able to share it all with you in this book. Here are some of the most important things you need to know before you get started:

- ✦ There is no right or wrong way to read tarot. This book has been written to inspire and support you on your journey, not dictate what you should or shouldn't do.

- ✦ There are no correct keywords or meanings for each card. The expanded card meanings chapter is a blend of traditional meanings and my own empowered meanings and understanding of the energy of the cards. If the cards mean something totally different to you then that is what they mean to you.

- ✦ Card readings should always be empowering and supportive. I hear all sorts of horror stories – I have some myself! – about people having experienced disempowering, disappointing and even scary readings with the tarot. You'll find none of that in this book. I only ever read tarot for myself and others to uplift, support and empower you to live your best and highest life.

- ✦ The scary cards aren't really that scary once you get to know them.

- ✦ Predictions are only ever potentials, never absolutes. The tarot can't tell you what's going to happen and it doesn't create your fate: you do! Fortune telling is over; now, we're carving out our own destinies.

me on my spiritual journey, and for helping me to live more deeply, truthfully, powerfully and peacefully. Thank you that every reading done with these cards will always be in alignment with love, light, my best and highest good and the best and highest good of those I read for. And so it is.'

✦ Go through the cards, touching each one while holding the intention that this deck will help you receive the highest guidance.

✦ Pull some cards on a question that's in your heart or mind.

✦ Put the cards back in the deck, then shuffle the deck and place it on your altar with a crystal on top or put it back in the box and keep it somewhere safe.

Storing your tarot deck

There is an old tarot tradition that says the best way to store a deck is to take it out of the box, wrap it in a silk scarf and keep it in a wooden box. This isn't such a great way of storing decks if you have more than a few, like to travel with them, want to be able to grab one quickly when you have a burning question or if you're vegan: silk isn't vegan friendly!

There are no rules, but do try to store your deck in a respectful way. Don't throw your cards around, leave them under piles of junk, forget them in the bottom of your bag for months on end or let the dog eat them. Trust your intuition and look after your decks however feels right for you. Just remember to care for them as the sacred tools they are.

KEEPING A TAROT JOURNAL

In this book you'll find lots of invitations to pull a card or for some tarot time. Whenever you come across these sections, write down which cards you pulled and what those cards meant for you in the moment and anything else that comes up for you.

Tarot journalling is a powerful part of the process of becoming a more confident tarot reader. You do not need anything fancy or special for your tarot journal. You can use a plain old notebook, exercise or composition book or you can even use your computer or notes app on your phone. My favourite tarot journal is an A4 spiral notebook. I love that I can easily flip to the next page and there is no pressure to keep it neat and perfect.

FOR EACH ENTRY IN YOUR TAROT JOURNAL WRITE:

✦ the date

✦ the phase of the moon or other important astrological alignments

✦ your emotional state: relaxed, tired, hopeful, under the weather and so on

✦ the deck you used

✦ the question/s you asked

✦ your thoughts, feelings or anything else that comes to mind for each card. If you need to go to the expanded card meanings chapter, include only what feels relevant from that section.

Introduction to the tarot system

KEEPING A JOURNAL CAN HELP YOU:

+ Make sense of your reading.
+ Develop your intuition: each time you write about the cards without checking to see what they mean first you are practising working with your intuition.
+ Develop a deeper connection with your guides. You may even find you start channelling messages from them as you write.
+ Notice patterns in your readings or cards that always show up.
+ See how things are unfolding and evolving over time.
+ Remember your readings.
+ Check back and see how accurate your readings are.

If journalling is not for you, do try to find some way of recording your readings. Take photos of the cards you pull, keep voice notes for yourself or create a private social media account where you share your photos and thoughts on your readings just for you and a few close friends.

THE FOLLOWING QUESTIONS MAY GIVE YOU DEEPER INSIGHTS WITH YOUR TAROT JOURNALLING:

+ How does this card make me feel?
+ What's the first thing that pops into my head when I see this card?
+ Do I have any resistance to this card and, if so, why might this be?

- ✦ Are any uncomfortable emotions or thoughts coming up? How can I move through these?
- ✦ What would happen if I took this guidance and followed it?
- ✦ What could I do to take a step towards or away from this potential outcome?
- ✦ What action am I being called to take here?

Tarot time!

Go through your tarot deck and choose two cards: one you like the most that you'd love to see come up for you in a reading, and one you like the least that you never want to see in your readings. Journal on the following questions for both of these cards:

- ✦ What do I like/dislike about this card (colour, image, keywords and so on)?
- ✦ How does it make me feel?
- ✦ Does this card bring up any memories?
- ✦ Where do I feel this in my body?
- ✦ Does this card remind me of someone in my life?
- ✦ What situation in my past lives or present one could this card relate to?
- ✦ If I saw this card in a reading right now, what guidance would it have for me?

Introduction to the tarot system

WHO ARE YOU CONNECTING WITH?

Getting clear on who you are communicating or connecting with when you do a tarot reading can make a huge difference when it comes to getting clear readings. It's so simple, yet many people never think about this aspect of card reading. How often do you hear phrases such as 'I'll ask the cards' or 'The cards told me . . .'? It's not really the cards that are speaking to you, it's who or what you are communicating with *through* the cards that is giving you guidance.

You can use the tarot to connect with:

- ✦ your subconscious mind
- ✦ your inner knowing
- ✦ your higher self
- ✦ spirit guides
- ✦ gods or goddesses
- ✦ angels and archangels
- ✦ ascended masters
- ✦ ancestors
- ✦ the universe
- ✦ any other type of inner or higher guidance.

Using the word 'guides' can be a simple, all-encompassing way to call on those who guide you. For ease, in this book I've used the word 'guides' to encompass whoever or whatever it is you are calling upon when reading the cards, but feel free to use this interchangeably with intuition, angels, inner knowing and so on.

This short ritual will help you open the channel of communication between you and your guides or whoever you would like to be open to receiving guidance from:

+ Hold the cards in your hands and close your eyes.

+ Take three deep breaths.

+ Concentrate on who or what you'd like to connect with.

+ Say mentally or out loud:
  'Thank you [whoever you want to connect with] for being with me as I do this reading and for showing me the cards that will most guide me right now.'

+ You can then ask a more specific question such as 'What do I most need to know about . . .?', or just ask for general guidance.

+ Shuffle the cards and choose the card you most feel drawn to.

+ Take a moment to sit with the card you pulled and consider how it answers your question and what guidance you are being given.

+ When you're done, always thank whoever it was you called in to help you. A simple 'Thank you, guides' is sufficient.

Whenever you read cards, always set an intention before you start pulling cards for who you'd like to communicate with.

PREPARING YOUR SPACE FOR A READING

You can read tarot cards anywhere, but it can bring another level to your readings if you can create a safe, sacred space in which to do your readings. Your reading space can be anywhere from sitting at your altar, on the back porch, the edge of your bed or the kitchen table: what makes a space sacred is your intention.

Try this simple ritual to prepare your space for a reading:

✦ Physically clean and clear the space.

✦ Light some incense or herbs and waft them around the space, spritz an aura spray or visualise white light clearing through the space.

✦ Place a reading cloth down – this can be a tablecloth, simple scarf or bandana – light a candle, play some relaxing music, place your crystals around you and get comfortable.

All of this can help you get into the right mental and spiritual energy for your tarot reading, but it isn't essential. As long as you have your cards and a positive intention you can do a reading anywhere and at any time.

Preparing Your Energy for a Reading

Being relaxed and centred before you start a reading will give you a clearer, more grounded reading. Just like you may not be in the best place to communicate with a partner or friend when you're angry, frustrated, overly emotional or unfocused or distracted, it's also not always the best time to do a tarot reading for yourself. However, there are plenty of ways you can prepare your energy to help you get into the right energetic place and head space for tarot reading.

Clear your energy: energy-clearing practices can help you release any negativity you've picked up or that has been sent to you or you've created within yourself before you read the cards. It's also a chance to clear the thoughts, opinions or ideas of other people you've picked up that may influence the reading.

✦ Visualise white light coming down into your crown chakra at the top of

Introduction to the tarot system

your head and moving down through your chakra column, down your legs and into your feet. Visualise this light expanding all around you, clearing your entire auric field.

✦ Spritz an aura spray or waft incense or smoke from sage or palo santo through your aura.

✦ Wash your hands.

✦ Take a deep inhale and exhale.

✦ Affirm 'I am clear' three times.

Protect your energy: protecting your energy before a reading helps keep you safe and aligned with only the messages from the guides who have your best and highest good at heart.

✦ Visualise a bubble or shield of white or blue light around you.

✦ Visualise a circle of white light around you and the space.

✦ Hold or wear a protective crystal: smoky quartz, black onyx, black tourmaline or anything dark is great for protection.

✦ Ask your guides or angels to protect you in the space.

✦ Affirm 'I am protected' three times.

Ground your energy: being ungrounded can be one of the biggest blocks to getting a clear reading, because if your energy is all over the place it will be much harder to understand the messages in the cards. Grounding practices are all about getting back into your body and into the present moment so you can receive the guidance you need.

- ✦ Visualise roots growing out of your feet and into the earth beneath you.
- ✦ Keep both feet on the ground during a reading.
- ✦ Eat something grounding and avoid caffeine, sugar and alcohol before reading.
- ✦ Carry, wear or hold dark or earthy-toned crystals while you read: try moss agate, tree agate or petrified wood.
- ✦ Affirm 'I am grounded' three times.

TRY THIS SIMPLE RITUAL TO PREPARE YOURSELF FOR A READING:

- ✦ Clear and set up your space.
- ✦ Close your eyes and take a few deep breaths. Visualise a golden white light pouring down into the top of your head and clearing your body and energy field. Affirm 'I am clear' three times.
- ✦ Visualise a bright blue shield of protective light all around you. Affirm 'I am protected' three times.
- ✦ Visualise roots growing out of your feet and into the earth below you. Affirm 'I am grounded' three times.
- ✦ Call in your guides and thank them for being with you and guiding you in the reading.
- ✦ State your intention, such as: 'May everything that comes through in this reading be in alignment with my best and highest good.'

Introduction to the tarot system

TAROT READING BASICS

In this chapter you'll learn how to shuffle and pull cards, and we'll go deeper into some important topics such as predictions, reversals and the scary cards.

SHUFFLING

There is no right or wrong way to shuffle your tarot cards: it's all about finding what works best for you. Here are some options to get you started:

✦ The waterfall or overhand shuffle: hold the deck in one hand and then with the other lift up sections of the deck from behind and place them back in front with your other hand.

✦ Riffle or casino shuffle: split the deck, holding half of the cards in each hand. Riffle the corners of each half of the deck together before bringing the cards back into a full deck, cutting again and repeating the process. While this is a very effective shuffling technique, it can cause your cards to get a little dog-eared and damaged.

- ✦ The piling shuffle: cut the deck, make three piles and place the piles back together again in a different order. Keep going until you feel the cards are shuffled.
- ✦ Smooshing: spread the cards out on a table or the floor and then start smooshing or swirling them around before bringing them back into a deck.

CHOOSING TAROT CARDS

Figuring out which cards to pick or pull during a reading is an intuitive process that will become easier each time you read. Here are some options:

- ✦ The intuitive waterfall: shuffle using the waterfall shuffle described above. Focus on your question and wait for a card to stick out from the pack.
- ✦ The fan feel: spread the deck out in a fan shape on your reading cloth. Let your hand hover over the cards until you feel or see a card that calls to you. You can also use a pendulum for this and watch for it to start moving over a card that wants your attention.
- ✦ The three-pack split: shuffle in whatever way you like. When you are done place the pack face down, cut the deck into three and bring the pack back together in a different order. Place the cards down into your spread in order from the top of the deck.

Try different methods to see what works for you.

Tarot reading basics

JUMPING CARDS OR FLIERS

When a card jumps or flies out of the deck, pay attention! You can add fliers into your spread or consider them as extra-important additional messages. You can also simply take note of the card and put it back into the deck and keep shuffling. You may be surprised at how often those cards will appear in your reading.

Note: if a bunch of cards fly out all at once it could simply be a message to work on your shuffling technique.

PLACING CARDS DOWN

Traditionally tarot cards are shuffled, chosen and placed face down in a spread. When turning your cards over, turn from left to right so that the original orientation of the card remains. You can choose to turn one card over at a time, taking time to look at each message – this is easiest for beginners – or turn them all over at once and look at the big picture straight away. You will find which way works best for you.

HOW TO ASK QUESTIONS

Some types of questions work better for tarot readings than others, but do remember that you are asking your guides and not the cards. Avoid questions that give away your power and free will such as asking what you 'should' do. A good way to frame any question is: 'What do I most need to know about [a particular situation]?'

Always ask one question at a time. If there are a few things on your mind, then do separate readings. They all may end up being connected as things often are, but asking one clear question per reading will always give clearer results. Asking clear questions is the best way to get clear answers!

READING FOR PREDICTIONS

Predictive readings, or fortune-telling, has been a very popular form of divination in the past, but times are changing and we're much more aware these days of just how much power we have to manifest and create our future. Tarot reading can help you look ahead at what *may* be coming or show you a potential outcome if you stay on a particular course, but asking to see your future and blindly accepting it as truth isn't the way of the empowered modern mystic. Instead of asking about your future, ask for guidance about how you can create the best future for yourself.

Predictive readings can have the potential to create fear, anxiety and hopelessness if the outcome you're shown isn't what you hoped for or wanted. The worst-case scenario can be that you end up manifesting or creating an unwanted outcome through your own beliefs and subconscious actions. Predictive readings can end up becoming a self-fulfilling prophecy. When reading for outcomes remember you're only being shown a *potential* outcome. You always have the power to change things: the cards don't dictate your fate, your actions and choices do.

Whether or not you decide to do predictive readings for yourself is totally up to you. Some people do find predictions helpful, like getting a heads-up, knowing what to look out for or what to change to avoid something they don't want. Other people prefer to use their tarot cards as a way to look at the here and now and make plans for the future they most want. If you do decide to do predictive readings, don't ever forget your power.

READING WITH REVERSALS

Reading using reversed cards can bring more information into a reading but it's not essential, especially if you find you're already getting plenty of guidance from just reading the cards upright. It really comes down to personal choice. To shuffle your cards for reading reversals you'll want to have about half the deck upright and half reversed.

- ✦ Use the smooshing shuffle.
- ✦ Hold the deck in one hand, press the fingers of your other hand onto the top of the deck and begin to spin the cards in a circle.
- ✦ Shuffle and cut the deck. Turn one pile upside down, then add it back to the deck and continue shuffling.

There are many ways to read reversed cards. Here are some things to consider when you see your cards appear upside down:

- ✦ Read the opposite of the upright meaning; for example, the Ace of Cups upright can suggest a full cup while reversed it can suggest an empty one.

- The energy may be stuck or blocked and unable to flow; for example, The Sun upright can suggest happiness and joy while reversed it could mean that there is something blocking your ability to feel and connect with that happiness.
- Reversals can show resistance; for example, the Six of Swords upright can show moving on from a difficult situation while reversed it can suggest you have resistance to moving on.
- Reversals can show potential; for example, if The Magician is reversed it can show there is a potential here for you to step into the energy of The Magician and take back your power, but you're not yet reaching it.
- Reversed cards can show your shadow aspects or things you are not yet willing and ready to accept about yourself or your situation.
- Reversed cards can show you a challenge to overcome or something you need to work on within yourself.

REPEATING CARDS

Sometimes known as 'stalker' cards, repeating cards are those that show up repeatedly in your readings. These cards are definitely trying to tell you something! Repeating cards can mean:

- This is an important lesson for you right now.
- This is a place that needs focus when it comes to your personal development and/or spiritual journey.

- ✦ You're not yet getting the message your guides are trying to give you about this card. You can use a clarifier card (see below) to get more information if you don't know what they are trying to tell you.
- ✦ This is part of your soul growth or higher purpose.

Tarot time!

When you get a repeating card and can't make sense of it, try this spread:

- ✦ The repeating card (place this out in front).
- ✦ What is this card trying to tell you?
- ✦ What are you not seeing?
- ✦ What is the lesson here?
- ✦ How you can get the message and move on.

CLARIFYING CARDS

Clarifying cards or clarifiers are extra cards pulled any time during a reading to gain more clarity in the reading. Usually they are pulled after looking at a reading in full if you want more information about a specific card. You can use clarifiers to:

✦ make sense of one specific card in a reading
✦ help you get unstuck and figure out a message that's evading you
✦ provide more information or detail on one card
✦ create deeper meaning when the clarifier and original cards are blended together
✦ ask a second question about something that comes up in the reading
✦ expand on and evolve the reading in a different direction.

Try to avoid pulling too many clarifiers: one should be enough. If it's not, check the troubleshooting chapter at the end of the book.

THE 'SCARY' CARDS

There are some cards in the deck that can feel a little scary to come across in your readings, especially at the beginning of your journey with the tarot. Please know that there is absolutely nothing to fear when these cards come up in a reading and, in fact, they can often signal huge positive change in your life.

If you've ever experienced a jolt of fear or feeling of unease at seeing one of the so-called scary cards pop up this is totally normal, and it doesn't mean you won't be able to get past it and start to see those cards as powerful guides on your journey. You can look through the expanded meanings section of this book for more information about the scary cards, but here's a quick guide to some of these more challenging cards so you can leave fear behind right from the start.

✦ **Death:** the Death card signifies endings, change and transition. When this card appears in a reading it's showing you that something needs to change, that the old needs to go so the new can live. In some decks you'll see this card as death and rebirth. The death card doesn't just signify the end of something: it is the closing of one chapter so that a new one can start. It can show the end of something, but only as part of a bigger transitional period.

✦ **The Tower:** The Tower is actually the card of enlightenment. You will sometimes see an eye depicted on this card along with a flash of lightning. The Tower brings a realisation of what's not working or of what's no longer in alignment. It shows you that the old way of doing things and seeing the world is no longer going to work. You can think of the crumbling tower as all the things that are not in alignment with your heart and soul being cleared so you can rebuild a life of deeper meaning.

✦ **The Devil:** this is a tricky one for anyone who has grown up in a Christian household or culture. The Devil card has nothing to do with a literal Christian devil but is a metaphor for the chains that bind you. The Devil card shows you where you are keeping yourself in chains, stuck in your mindset, habits or actions and the stories you tell yourself. This card brings an opportunity to break those chains and take back your power.

✦ **Judgement:** usually depicting imagery of a Christian rapture, this is a card of spiritual awakening and ascension. Judgement can appear when you are learning, growing and evolving spiritually or when you are being asked to go further on that journey. It can also symbolise literal judgement, showing you whether you are being too hard on yourself or others.

✦ **Three of Swords:** often called the card of heartbreak, the Swords suit relates to thoughts and ideas more than emotions. The Three of Swords can remind you that it's often your own thoughts that are causing you the most distress and that you have the power to change your thoughts and create a different experience for yourself. You can choose to see this as a card of healing rather than suffering: the swords have already done their damage, and now the job is to begin the healing journey.

✦ **Nine of Swords:** this card represents your fears, worry and anxiety. The Nine of Swords is not telling you there's anything to worry *about*, though; in fact, it's usually highlighting that your worry is the real issue rather than any event or situation that may or may not occur.

✦ **Ten of Swords:** seeing all those swords sticking out of the figure's back on this card can be a little unnerving, but it

Tarot reading basics

simply signifies endings and especially the end of a difficult situation or karmic cycle. Something has come full circle, lessons have been learned, karma has been transmuted and now it's time to rest and heal before the new cycle begins.

The tarot contains 78 cards that mirror life experiences. There will always be times in life that are more challenging the others, but when you really understand what the scary cards are trying to show you, you can navigate these challenges with so much more ease and power. If a scary card comes up in a reading and you feel thrown by it, pull a clarifying card and ask a second question to get more information and see the positive in the situation. Here are some examples:

✦ **Death:** what do I need to let go of so I can move into a new chapter?
✦ **The Tower:** what is no longer serving or supporting me?
✦ **The Devil:** how can I break these chains?
✦ **Judgement:** what is awakening within me?
✦ **Three of Swords:** what needs healing, and how can I support myself on this healing journey?
✦ **Nine of Swords:** which of my fears are unfounded?
✦ **Ten of Swords:** what challenging cycle is ending for me now?

If you pull a scary card in a potential outcome position, pull another card to ask what you can do to change the outcome into something more positive.

Pull a card!

Pull a card and ask the question: 'How can the scary cards serve and support me on my tarot journey?'

Scary card tip: if you still find that pulling a scary card gives you a feeling of dread you can take them out of your deck, at least while you're just starting out. As you feel more comfortable and gain a better understanding of these cards you can slowly bring them back in to make a full deck.

Tarot reading basics

NEXT STEPS

In this chapter you'll learn how to develop your intuition and gain insights into numerology, astrology and other systems that can give more depth to you readings.

DEVELOPING INTUITION

There is so much more to reading the tarot than just memorising someone else's keywords and meanings. Tarot is an intuitive art, and while the meanings in this book can get you started you don't need to rely on them to get clear, insightful readings.

Getting clear guidance

There are four main ways in which your guides or inner knowing will communicate with you during your readings: these are the clairs, with 'clair' meaning 'clear'. You may have one main way of receiving or intuiting guidance or be able to work with two or even all of the ways listed below. As you practise reading for yourself you'll begin to deepen your understanding of how your guidance speaks to you.

Clairvoyance

Clairvoyance or clear seeing is the most well-known way to receive guidance. During your readings you may find that you get most of your guidance from the imagery, symbols or colours on the card. Clairvoyants usually excel at visualisation, will absolutely love pathworking (see page 67) and may be able to see vivid and detailed scenes coming to life through meditating on the cards. If you turn over a tarot card and find yourself seeing visions or images in your inner eye, even things that don't appear on the card, you may be clairvoyant.

YOU CAN DEVELOP YOUR CLAIRVOYANCE BY:

✦ working with the pathworking activities on pages 67 and 68

✦ sitting in meditation and letting your gaze rest on the card's image, being open to whatever comes through

✦ practising visualisation in any form such as reading fiction, guided meditations and so on.

Clairaudience

Clairaudience is clear hearing, and it involves hearing your guidance through sounds, words, phrases or music. If you turn over a tarot card and a song starts playing in your head or if you hear words or phrases clearly cutting through your thoughts, that may be clairaudient guidance. Clairaudient guidance will always be loving, kind, supportive and helpful. If you are hearing any voices that do not feel loving or kind, always seek help from a professional.

YOU CAN DEVELOP YOUR CLAIRAUDIENCE BY:

✦ making a tarot playlist by choosing a song for each card, then when you need guidance hit shuffle and play

✦ listening to any playlist on shuffle or put the radio on and listen for lyrics that really jump out and speak to you

✦ paying attention to any words or phrases that come to mind when reading the cards.

Clairsentience

Clairsentience or clear feeling involves receiving intuitive guidance through your physical body and emotions. Notice how you feel emotionally when you turn over the cards. You may also feel physical sensations during readings, although these should pass quickly if they are connected with clairsentience. Always check out any unusual physical issues you're concerned about.

YOU CAN DEVELOP YOUR CLAIRSENTIENCE BY:

+ listening to your body
+ paying attention to your emotions
+ going through the tarot deck and noticing where you feel each card in your body
+ considering the emotions that the cards bring up.

Claircognizance

Claircognizance is clear knowing, and if this is your way of receiving guidance you'll just *know* what the messages are in a reading. It can take some time and practice to be able to tell the difference between your thoughts and clear guidance, but one way to tell is that your guidance will always be clearer and more direct than your regular thoughts and always loving, even if it's tough loving!

YOU CAN DEVELOP YOUR CLAIRCOGNIZANCE BY:

✦ thinking about times when you just *knew* something and remembering how it felt at the time

✦ paying attention to your thoughts and ideas

✦ always asking yourself what you think a card means first before looking up its meaning

✦ trusting your inner knowing instead of second-guessing yourself.

Developing the clairs

Developing your clairs, psychic ability and intuition can take time. You can always use the expanded card meanings chapter to help guide your readings, but before you do take a moment to just sit and consider what you think or feel the messages are for you first. Any time you pull a card, consider these questions:

✦ What's the first thing you notice about this card: does something in the image grab your attention?

✦ Do any words, phrases or song lyrics come to mind?

✦ How do you feel about this card?

✦ What do *you* think the card means in this situation?

Pull a card!

Prepare your energy, shuffle your tarot deck and ask the question: 'What do I most need to know about developing my psychic ability and intuition?'

Creating your own keyword meanings

A fantastic practice for developing intuition is to create your own keywords and meanings for your tarot deck.

Tarot time!

Put your deck in order and grab your journal, then:

- ✦ Quickly turn over the first card and write the first thing that comes to you: no pausing or second-guessing yourself, as it doesn't matter how wild or disconnected from the traditional meanings it is. Just write that first thing down.
- ✦ Put the card aside and go onto the next card.
- ✦ Continue until you've gone through the whole deck.

The trick with this exercise is to do it quickly so you can get out of your own way. You can even set a timer for yourself for four or five minutes to help you keep pace.

If you come across a card and nothing comes through, instead of forcing something or looking at the expanded card meanings chapter put the card in a second pile and go back to it at the end. Don't worry if at the end you have some gaps in your list: this isn't about perfection, it's about freeing your intuition.

After you've done this exercise you will have a whole list of keywords and phrases that you can use in your readings. You may find some are similar to those in this book while some may be completely different, but it's all good. In fact, it's great if you see something totally different in the cards because it means you're really using your intuition!

This is a good practice to revisit often, as different words and ideas will come to you each time you do this.

Next steps

NUMEROLOGY

Each of the numbers from 1 to 10 has a specific energy and vibration that bring more depth to your understanding of each minor card and the majors from 1 to 10 and 11 and 22. The other major cards can be added down to single digits or read as two numbers; for example, The Hanged Man (12) can be read as both a 10 and a 2 or you can add 1 + 2 to get 3.

1 (ace)	The self and individuality, new beginnings, potential, independence, manifestation	7	Spirituality, knowledge, wisdom, luck, perseverance
2	Duality, partnerships, balance, alignment	8	Abundance, prosperity, transformation, infinity, personal power
3	Creativity, collaboration, growth, expansion, teamwork	9	Accomplishment, contentment, rewards, success
4	Stability, structure, maturity, order, leadership	10	Completion, culmination, lessons learned, transcendence, consolidation, chapters ending
5	Change, challenge, conflict, unpredictability	11	The illuminator, spiritual awareness, enlightenment, higher purpose
6	Love, beauty, harmony, generosity, victory	22	The master builder, manifesting on a grand scale, leadership, harmony between the material and spiritual planes

THE ELEMENTS

Every card in the tarot has an elemental correspondence, all of which are included in the expanded meanings section. Understanding how the elements are at play in the tarot can bring another layer to your interpretations of the cards and your readings as a whole. The minors are heavily influenced by the element of their suit.

ELEMENT/SUIT	POSITIVE	NEGATIVE
Fire/Wands	Solar plexus chakra, willpower, courage, passion, desire, action, projective, balanced masculine, making things happen	Burnout, frustration, anger, aggression
Water/Cups	Sacral and heart chakras, emotions, intuition, psychic awareness, sensitivity, relationships, love, receptive, feminine, calm, soothing, dreamy	Illusions, overly emotional, drowning in your own sorrows
Air/Swords	Throat and crown chakras, thoughts, ideas, mindset, clarity, self-expression, truth, spirit, cleansing	Overthinking, overanalysing, overwhelm, anxiety, abrasive, cutting or hurtful communication
Earth/Pentacles	Root chakra, material world, money, finances, work, abundance, grounding, physical body	Tired, stuck, stagnant, sluggish, unable to move forward, unhealthy obsession with money and success

Next steps

Tarot time!

Seeing an abundance of one minor suit in a reading can indicate a need to pay attention to that element and how it's working in your life. Prepare your energy, then do a reading for yourself using any of the spreads in this book. See how many cards of each suit appear in your reading and note the following:

✦ **Mostly Wands:** be courageous and take action to create the outcome you most want. Avoid getting too fired up over the situation.

✦ **Mostly Cups:** listen to your feelings and trust your intuition. Other people may be involved and can also help you get through this. Try to avoid getting overly emotional about this situation.

✦ **Mostly Swords:** your thoughts may be having more impact than you realise. Pay close attention to stories you are telling yourself.

✦ **Mostly Pentacles:** this indicates a need to show up and do the work in order to get the outcome you most desire. Stay grounded, but don't be too focused on the material otherwise you'll lose sight of things that are important.

✦ **Mostly majors:** big things are happening such as awakenings, initiations, transformations, life changes, spiritual growth or calls to your highest destiny.

COURT CARDS AND THEIR ELEMENTS

The court cards have two elements working with them: the element of their suit and the element of their role in court.

Pages/earth: youth, study, exploration. The Pages are the youngest members of the court and have youthful enthusiasm for life, and they represent new beginnings and fresh starts. The Pages often represent children and young people. They are the students of the court and can show you where you still need to learn and grow.

Knights/air: action, movement, service. The Knights are the action takers. They have finished their study and now they are off to do their work in the world by taking charge and moving towards their goals and purpose. They also often work for and on behalf of others.

Queens/water: creativity, feminine, receptive. The Queens are mature leaders who represent the feminine, creative, intuitive and receptive energy of their element.

Kings/fire: mastery, masculine, success. The Kings represent masculine, projective, organising aspects. They have achieved success and full mastery over their element.

Next steps   59

ASTROLOGY

Every card in the tarot has an astrological correspondence. Each major card has either a planetary or zodiacal correspondence, the minors have both a celestial body and a zodiac sign and the court cards correspond with astrological signs. Pages represent pure potential so they correspond with all the zodiac signs associated with their element; Knights are assigned to the mutable signs as they are changeable and adventurous; Queens correspond to the cardinal signs, those that appear at the beginning of a new season; and Kings correspond to the grounded, hard-working fixed signs of the zodiac.

Tarot time!

Take some time to go through the expanded meanings later in this book and find the cards in the major, minor and court card sections that correspond with your zodiac sign. If you know your rising sign you can find those cards as well. Take these cards out of your deck and journal on each one, asking:

✦ How does this card make me feel?
✦ How does this card relate to me and my journey right now?
✦ What are the positive aspects of this card to embody?
✦ What are the aspects to work on and overcome?

IMAGERY AND SYMBOLISM

There are some common symbols that appear often in the tarot, and having an idea of some of the traditional meanings of these symbols can be useful in going more deeply in your interpretations during readings.

Next steps

SYMBOL	MEANING	SYMBOL	MEANING
Red rose	Wisdom, passion, desire, life force, physical love, material or physical realm	Moon	Subconscious, intuition, mystery, illusion, cycles, dreams, hidden aspects
White rose	Purity, innocence, spirituality, divine love, spiritual realm	Star	Hope, inspiration, divine guidance, wisdom, light in the darkness
White lily	Compassion, purity, faith, divine love and truth, transformation, death and rebirth	Snake, serpent	Wisdom, knowledge, transformation, temptation, kundalini energy
Yod*	Divine presence, divine spark, blessings or inspiration, potential, cosmic order, divine plan	Crown	Authority, power, enlightenment, mastery, leadership
Pillar	Duality, balance, portals or gateways between states of consciousness, portals between the physical and spiritual realms, portals between the known and unknown	Laurel wreath	Victory, success, goals reached, achievement
Mountain	Challenges, goals, aspirations, obstacles, obstacles overcome, spiritual attainment	Trees, greenery	Tree of life, growth, abundance, fertility, grounding, stability, wisdom
Water, river, waterfall	Intuition, subconscious, emotions, spiritual realm, flow of life, nourishment	Bird	Freedom, divine messengers, higher or broader perspective, rising above challenges, vision
Sun	Life force, vitality, joy, enlightenment, strength, success, revealing truths		

*Small flames that often appear to fall from the sky in the tarot.

ADVANCING YOUR READINGS

In this chapter you will discover advanced tarot practices from pathworking and spells to shadow work and past-life readings.

INTUITIVE READING

Many people focus on memorising keyword meanings when they first start out reading tarot. This method has its place, but practising intuitive reading is the best way to get to the next level with your readings. Listed below are some ways you can dive even deeper into intuitive reading:

✦ Put all your books out of reach – including this one – so you have to rely on your own interpretations.

✦ Always pay attention to the first thing you think, feel, see or hear when you turn over each card in your spread.

✦ Keep notes of your intuitive readings and come back to them later to see how accurate and resonate they were.

✦ Give yourself permission to see what *you* see in the cards: if you see or feel something that doesn't relate at all to the traditional meanings, trust it!

✦ Create your own deck: draw, paint or use collage, whatever works for you, to create your own tarot deck. This is one of the most fun and powerful ways to develop your intuition and deepen your connection with the cards.

PATHWORKING

Pathworking can help you gain deeper insights into the energy of the cards and can be done with both the majors and minors of the deck, but if you're just starting out work only with the majors as they have more symbolism and are much more interesting journeys to take. Start with a major card that you feel is positive: a card that you like seeing in your readings. The Magician, The Empress, The Star or even The Hermit will work well for your first time pathworking.

THIS IS THE PATHWORKING PROCESS:

✦ Choose your card and put it down in front of you.

✦ Sit in a comfortable meditative position.

✦ Take three slow deep breaths.

✦ Open your eyes and look at the card in front of you.

✦ Imagine that you are entering the card: see yourself stepping into the frame and into the scene.

✦ Take a few moments to explore the scene from all angles.

✦ Notice how you feel while being inside this card: what feelings does it bring up for you?

✦ If there is a figure in the card, take a moment to speak with them and ask them any questions you may have. For example, you may like to ask The Magician for advice on how to do magic, ask The Empress how to give birth to your creative projects or ask The Star for some divine guidance.

Advancing your readings

67

- ✦ When you feel you've fully experienced the card, see yourself stepping back out of the card and into your body.
- ✦ Ground yourself by rubbing your feet on the floor and taking three more deep breaths.
- ✦ Write about what you experienced in your tarot journal.

Take time to do a pathworking practice every now and again. You can always come back and explore the same card again, as each time you do you will uncover new information about it.

NUMEROLOGY

Understanding more about numerology will not only help you in your tarot readings, but will also give you more insight into your psyche and life purpose through your life path card and support you in navigating collective energies of each year with the collective year card and personal year card.

Life path card

Your life path number is the number that has the most significance for you in this lifetime, and can help you understand yourself and see what your biggest challenges and lessons are. Traditional numerology and the tarot have many similarities, and you will easily see how your life path number fits into the major arcana of the tarot.

To work out your life path number, add up each number in your birthdate:

If your birthday is on 15 July 1995 your life path number would be:

1 + 5 + 7 + 1 + 9 + 9 + 5 = 37

Take the final two digits and add them together:

3 + 7 = 10 = Wheel of Fortune

and again:

1 + 0 = 1 = The Magician

Traditionally, life path numbers always add down to one digit unless they are 11, 22 or 33, as these are the master numbers. When using the tarot, if your first double digit is also one of the major arcana cards you can use both cards as your guides, but your single digit number relates to your life path in numerology and will be your main life path card.

Your life path card is a special teacher and guide for you in this lifetime, and can hold a clue to your life purpose. Pay special attention when this card appears in your readings. To work with your life path number and card:

✦ Pathwork the card, journeying into it for special messages for you.

✦ Journal on the strengths, challenges and lessons of the card.

✦ Look at the most positive aspects of the card and see that they are within you.

✦ See this card as your personal guide: sit with and meditate on it often.

✦ Call on the being in the card to guide you.

✦ Put the card on your altar or desk and consider it often.

✦ Embody and embrace this energy.

Advancing your readings

Collective year card

Work out the collective year card by adding the numbers in the year together; for example:

2 + 0 + 2 + 5 = 9 = the year of The Hermit

The collective year card can help you understand the collective energy of the current year and can show you collective lessons everyone is learning or challenges everyone is facing. Work out the collective year card and then journal on the following:

✦ What lessons does this card bring?

✦ What challenges does this card bring?

✦ What would it be best for me to work on this year?

✦ What goals could I achieve?

✦ What daily habit or spiritual practice could support me this year?

✦ What other support might I need this year?

✦ How can I support others this year?

Personal year card

Your personal year card will show you your lessons, challenges and strengths for the year. To work out your personal year card add your date and month of birth and the current year:

If your birthday is 17 July and the year is 2025:

1 + 7 + 7 + 2 + 0 + 2 + 5 = 24

2 + 4 = 6

Your personal year card is The Lovers.

You can either consider your personal year starting at the beginning of the year or on your birthday; that is, in the example above you could say your personal 6 year starts at the beginning of 2025 *or* on 17 July. You can decide which way works best for you.

Tarot time!

Go through your deck and bring out your life path card, collective year card and personal year card. If any double up, that energy will be very strong for you. Look at how these cards play or react with each other: is there a common theme in the cards? If you blend these cards together what is that energy like, and what story do they tell you?

Journal on each card with these questions:

✦ What is the lesson of this card?
✦ What is the gift of this card?
✦ How can this energy support me in getting where I want to be on my journey?

MANIFESTING

The tarot is the perfect magical tool for manifesting. Here are some simple ways to use your tarot cards to help manifest and attract what you desire:

- Do a reading using a spread that includes a potential outcome position. Pull all cards normally but choose the outcome card upright from the deck. Affirm in writing that the outcome you want *will* manifest.

- Perform a three-card spread choosing all cards upright from the deck to represent your past and present and the future you most desire. Journal on this reading as if you had pulled the cards in a regular reading.

- Choose a card that represents what you want and put it somewhere you will see it often. Think of it as a mini vision board.

- Take a pathworking journey into a card that represents what you want to manifest. Feel yourself in that card and the card embodying all it represents to you.

- Take a photo of a card that represents what you want to manifest and set it as your phone screensaver.

TAROT SPELLS

Here are some simple ways to bring your cards into your magical workings:

- Always do a reading before a spell to make sure your spell work is aligned to your heart and highest good.

- When doing any kind of spell work place a tarot card representing your intention onto your altar or sacred space.

- Attune water, oils or any other magical item to the energies of a particular tarot card by placing them on top of a card. For example, place lemon oil over the Sun card for an extra boost of joy and vitality, place a pentagram pendant over the Ace of Pentagrams to attune it with the energy of new opportunities and prosperity.

- Clear, charge and activate crystals by placing them on top of cards that align with the energies you want those crystals to be attuned to. For example: place amethyst over the High Priestess for a boost of intuition or carnelian over the Empress to attune it with more potent creative energy.

Tarot candle spell

For this spell you will need a tarot card representing your intention, a candle (white works for anything; otherwise, choose a colour most prominent in the card you are using), something sharp so you can carve into your candle (a crystal point, earring back or drawing pin), an oil that matches your intention (you can use a specific oil mentioned later in this chapter or whatever you have that aligns with your purpose), a candle holder and matches or a lighter. Follow this procedure:

- Clear your space.
- Gather your supplies and set up your space.
- Prepare your energy by clearing, protecting and grounding yourself.

- Call in your guides, angels or any deities you work with or would like to support you. You can do this by simply saying: 'Thank you, guides, for being with me and guiding and protecting me in my spell work today.'

- Set your intention and bring it to mind or say it out loud. For example: 'I'm here at my altar to cast a spell for [your intention].'

- Place the tarot card on your altar, then meditate on it and on your intention. Get really clear in your mind and in your heart about what you want.

- Hold the candle at your heart and state your intention out loud. For example: 'May this candle be symbolic of the [description of what you want] I am now calling into my life.'

- Engrave a word, phrase or symbol into the candle that represents your intention. You can even use the name of the tarot card or any symbols from the card.

- Dress the candle with the oil, still focusing on your intention. If you want to call something into your life then rub the oil from the top down, and if you want to release something then rub the oil from the bottom upwards.

- Place the candle in the candle holder, light it and affirm what you want three times. For example: 'Money now comes to me!'

- Say: 'May this spell be cast under the law of grace. May it harm none and may the outcome be in alignment with my best and highest good. And so it is, and so it is, and so it is.' The law of grace protects you from casting a spell that may not serve you.

- Take a moment to sit and meditate on the energy of this spell.
- Thank your guides, angels and deities.
- Let the candle safely burn to the bottom. If you need to pause the candle, use a candle snuffer and relight it when you can.
- If your spell was to banish or release something get rid of the remaining wax immediately, ideally away from your own home. If your spell was to call something into your life keep the wax on your altar, plant it or dispose of it in whatever way you intuitively feel called.

TAROT TALISMANS

Working with tarot cards as talismans is powerful magic that brings the energy of the tarot cards into any areas of your life. Working with tarot talismans can result in dog-eared tarot cards, so you may like to buy a spare set of cards to work with in this way.

Here are some simple ways to use your tarot cards as talismans:

- For a positive home life, place a harmonious card such as The Empress or Temperance over a doorway or in communal areas.
- When you need extra strength and courage, keep the Strength card in your back pocket.
- Place a positive card under your pillow for better dreams. The Star, Temperance or The High Priestess can help you have intuitive and safe dreams.

- ✦ To help you stay organised and focused at work, place The Emperor or Eight of Pentacles on your desk.
- ✦ Place a prosperity card such as the Queen or King of Pentacles in your purse.
- ✦ When going on a date take the Two of Cups or The Lovers card along with you.
- ✦ If you've been feeling a little down, place The Sun card on your bathroom mirror.
- ✦ If you want people to leave you alone, carry The Hermit card with you.
- ✦ Use your imagination and intuition to come up with more ways of working with tarot talismans!

SHADOW WORK

'Shadow' is a word coined by psychologist Carl Jung, who referred to the shadow self as the parts of people they find it uncomfortable to identify with or the darker sides of their natures. This definition has changed slightly in modern use to include anything about people and their choices or lives they push down, ignore, disown or just find it hard to look at.

Shadow work involves being willing to look at those parts of yourself and bring them to the light. In shadow work you face your fears, acknowledge the parts of you that you dislike or hide, look at where you hold unforgiveness towards yourself or others, work with your negative ego and bring to light any suffering, pain,

trauma or anything that's been hidden so it can be seen, released, integrated, healed and/or accepted.

Shadow work is trending right now, but that doesn't make it right for you. If you are dealing with any kind of trauma it can be better to seek professional help rather than working with the tarot alone, but if you're feeling ready to face what can sometimes be uncomfortable truths then shadow work can help you to let go, move on and love and accept yourself in a much deeper way.

When something comes up in your shadow work that's uncomfortable and difficult to face you have three options:

- ✦ Accept the shadow aspect, having compassion for what you find, and love that part of yourself.
- ✦ Integrate the shadow aspect, taking time to listen, understand and allow this part of yourself to exist without judgement.
- ✦ Transform the shadow aspect. Not all shadow aspects need to be loved and integrated: sometimes they need to be transformed, let go and released. This can still be done with love and acceptance but also a willingness to change the story.

Pull a card!

Pull one to three cards on each of the following:

✦ What aspects of my shadow need love and acceptance?
✦ What aspects of my shadow need to be integrated?
✦ What aspects of my shadow need to be transformed?

Shadow work in tarot readings

When you read the tarot you will sometimes see things you don't want to see. The cards can give you great advice, but they can also mirror back to you your thoughts, behaviours and choices and this can be hard to see. No one wants to be called out by the tarot, but when this happens it's a perfect opportunity for shadow work!

When you see something you don't want to see in the cards it can be tempting to put the cards back and try again or ignore the guidance that comes through, but if you can sit in the discomfort of those spaces, be open to seeing the truth of a situation even if that truth is that you are creating this problem yourself and be willing to take responsibility for your choices and actions, that's when you *really* have the power to make change in your life!

Here are some tips on how to deal with uncomfortable cards and messages that sometimes come up in your readings:

+ Take a deep breath and ground your energy. It's so much easier to look at difficulties when you're grounded.

+ Take a moment. Sometimes when challenging cards come up you immediately block your intuition, going into fear or resistance, but by taking a moment to move past those feelings you can see the reading more clearly.

+ Remember that difficult cards in your reading can sometimes be the *best* cards to see to help you on your best path.

+ When you see that you are creating a problem in your life, try to see this as a good thing. If you've created this problem it means you can also create the solution.

+ Remember that tarot readings are just showing you what you need to see at a certain point. This reading doesn't define you as a person; it's just what is needed to see in this moment.

+ When the cards call you out, see it as an opportunity for spiritual and personal growth and be grateful for it.

PAST-LIFE READINGS

The tarot is an excellent tool for looking into past lives. Knowing who you were in a past life and what challenges you faced then can help you see what stories or patterns may be replaying in your current life. Past-life readings give you an opportunity to release and let go of any old karma, beliefs, ancient vows or anything that may be affecting you in your current life.

When you first begin using your tarot for past-life work you may receive only general guidance and advice, but as you continue to develop your intuition and clairvoyance you may find that you're able to see past lives playing out in your mind's eye and work much more in depth with this process. Try this past-life tarot spread:

+ **Card 1:** who were you?

+ **Card 2:** where was this life? Look for clues in the image; for example, near water, in the desert and so on.

+ **Card 3:** what was your main purpose for incarnating in this time and place?

+ **Card 4:** what was your biggest obstacle in this life?

+ **Card 5:** what was your biggest lesson in this life?

+ **Card 6:** what was your biggest blessing in this life?

+ **Card 7:** what are you holding on to from this life?

+ **Card 8:** how is this life affecting you now?

+ **Card 9:** how can you clear and release the negative aspects of this life?

+ **Card 10:** how can you invoke and embody the blessings and power of this life?

CRYSTALS, HERBS AND OILS

As you work with the expanded card meanings chapter you'll notice each card has a crystal, herb and oil correspondence. There are various ways you can work with these spiritual tools.

If a specific card shows up a lot for you or there's a card you want to embody or experience the energy of, it can be useful to draw on the tools corresponding with that card. This can be an ally to help you move through the lesson or activate the energy associated with that card.

Crystals

Working with crystals can help you amplify specific energies during your readings. To work with crystals in readings:

- ✦ Place crystals on your tarot deck to charge and activate it before a reading.
- ✦ Place crystals on your deck to clear it after use.
- ✦ Hold or wear crystals whenever you do readings for yourself or others.
- ✦ Place crystals in your space or on your reading cloth to support the energy of the reading.

TRY THESE SPECIFIC CRYSTALS FOR TAROT READINGS:

✦ amethyst for intuition

✦ angelite for connecting with angels

✦ blue calcite for calm readings: it's helpful if you see that challenging cards are coming up

✦ citrine for confidence in your abilities

✦ clear quartz for clarity

✦ hematite for grounding

✦ rose quartz to help you stay heart-centred

✦ selenite for accessing higher consciousness

✦ smoky quartz for protection.

Herbs and oils

HERE ARE SOME IDEAS FOR WORKING WITH HERBS AND OILS:

✦ Use oils on candles and light them to activate or banish the energy of the card. This can be done with a simple statement; for example, 'I hereby banish the negative aspects of the Four of Cups from my being!' or 'I invoke the energy of the Nine of Pentacles into my life.' Use your own words and make this process yours.

✦ Dress the candle with herbs or burn herbs safely for the same purpose as above.

- Dab oil on a corner of the card to further activate the energy of it, but be careful as you don't want too much oil on your cards. Less is more!
- Use oil on personal items; for example, dab an oil corresponding to a positive Pentacles card onto your purse or wallet or your keycards or cash money. Do the same with the herbs that relate to the card: place them in your purse or wallet or wherever you intuitively feel called.
- Dab a diluted oil onto yourself to embody the energy of the card.
- Carry a little of a particular herb in your pocket as you go about your day; for example, carry The Emperor's herb for success at work or The Empress's herb for creativity.
- Use your imagination, as there are so many ways you can use these herbs and oils in your practices!

Important note: always be very careful when working with herbs, oils and fire. Check that herbs are non-toxic to pets and children if you are going to work with them for magical purposes and never digest them yourself. Always check that oils are safe to use on skin and always dilute them before applying.

READING FOR OTHERS

Once you have been reading confidently for yourself for some time you may feel called to read for others, but before you embark on what can be an incredibly rewarding side hustle or even career be sure to fully understand that this is a big responsibility. Your clients will share their deepest secrets, fears and dreams with you, and you not only need to be able to read their cards but you also need to be able to hold safe space for people going through difficult times.

WHEN READING FOR OTHERS:

✦ Always begin by clearing and grounding your energy and the space.

✦ Remain non-judgemental: whatever you think this person should do about their situation needs to be put aside so you can pass on the messages of higher guidance through the cards.

✦ Always keep confidentiality: never share anything about another person's reading.

✦ Never tell someone what to do: share what you see in the cards but make sure the querent feels empowered to make their own decisions.

✦ Read only for potential outcomes: never tell someone what is going to happen to them. They may make it happen if they believe strongly enough that it will.

✦ Always wish the best for those you are reading for.

✦ Clear your energy and space after a reading and thank your guides.

Pull a card!

Pull some cards on the following:

✦ What do I need to know about reading for others?
✦ Are there any blocks and challenges around me reading for others?
✦ How can I be an effective and empowering tarot reader for others?

FOLLOWING GUIDANCE AND TAKING ACTION

When it comes to advancing your tarot practice, the most important thing you can do is pay attention to the guidance you receive and take action where you are being called to. Many people read tarot for themselves and receive incredible insights but never use that guidance to make positive change in their lives. The tarot can help you change your life for the better in so many ways, but the cards can't sprout legs and do it for you. You are the one making the decisions in your life.

When you receive guidance, don't just write it in your journal and forget it: really listen to it, follow it, take action and see what happens! When you start to do this you'll find that the tarot is not just a tool for deep personal insight, but that it can guide you in living your best and highest life through the decisions you make and actions you take.

HERE ARE SOME TIPS TO HELP YOU FOLLOW THE GUIDANCE AND TAKE ACTION:

✦ At the end of each reading ask yourself 'What are my action steps?'
✦ Set an intention and make a plan for what you'll do with this guidance.
✦ Pay attention to what happens when you follow the guidance you're given, noticing how things change in your life for the better.
✦ Reward yourself for paying attention, showing up and taking action.

TAROT SPREADS

Working with tarot spreads can take you much more deeply into a question or situation by looking at various aspects and perspectives you may not be aware of or have considered. To work with a spread:

✦ Prepare your space and energy for a reading and call in your guides.

✦ Shuffle the cards, focusing on your question.

✦ Begin to draw cards and place them face down one at a time in the order and placement of the chosen spread.

✦ Turn each card over one at a time, focusing on how the card relates to your question and the prompt from each card's position.

✦ Journal on each card.

✦ If you need help understanding what the card means, pull a clarifying card.

✦ Continue until all of the cards are face up and have been read.

✦ Look at the reading as a whole. Are there common threads through the reading? Do you see cards with similar messages; for example, many of one suit? Notice how the cards blend together and what story they are telling you.

✦ Journal on the reading as a whole.

Complete the reading by thanking your guides and placing the cards back in the deck.

SIGNIFIERS

Some tarot spreads will ask you to place down a signifier, a card that is usually – although doesn't have to be – chosen face up to represent the querent or situation you are asking about. You can use the court card that corresponds with your sun sign or any other court card you most resonate with as a signifier. You can also use any signifier position as an extra card position in the spread to represent where you are in this current moment.

BLENDING CARDS

Being able to blend cards together to discover deeper meanings is a useful practice when reading with spreads. The cards all have relationships with each other and can talk to each other to create deeper meanings in your spreads.

Tarot time!

Pick two cards from the deck either upright or at random and read them together in a blended meaning. Do this quite a few times until you feel you are starting to get the hang of it then, when you are ready, practise with three cards or more. Here are some examples:

✦ Ace of Cups and Ten of Wands: a need to put yourself first so you don't burn out.

Tarot spreads

- ✦ The Hermit, Nine of Wands and Page of Swords: maintaining clarity of mind so you can stay the course with your spiritual development even when it's challenging.
- ✦ Five of Pentacles, The Magician and Ten of Cups: knowing that you have the power to change your story of struggle into one of abundance and happiness.

Pull two or three cards for yourself each day and practise blending them together in a specific personal reading.

Spread tip: look at your spread and notice in which direction the figures in the cards are facing or moving towards. For example, the Fool and the Hermit look towards the left and the Knight of Cups and Six of Swords move to the right. Pay extra attention to the cards that other cards seem to be moving towards. This can help you to understand the way energy is moving or can point towards the most important messages in the reading.

GENERAL SPREADS

In the following pages you'll
find spreads that can be used
with any question, issue,
situation or area of your life.

ONE-CARD SPREAD

A one-card reading is not technically a spread, but it's a great way to get some quick advice on any topic. Here are some simple ideas for questions for one-card readings:

- ✦ What do I most need to know right now?
- ✦ What do I need to focus on?
- ✦ What will help me move forward?
- ✦ What do I most need to know about . . . [a specific situation]?
- ✦ What energy could I embrace or embody?
- ✦ How can I walk my best and highest path today?

THREE-CARD SPREAD

There are many ways to work with three-card spreads; here are a few that can bring some quick guidance and support:

- **Card 1:** the past
- **Card 2:** the present
- **Card 3:** the potential outcome.

- **Card 1:** the current situation
- **Card 2:** blocks or challenges
- **Card 3:** how to move through this.

- **Card 1, your mind:** what's on your mind or what your mind needs
- **Card 2, your body:** material needs or messages from your body
- **Card 3, your spirit:** spiritual guidance.

ADVICE, ACTION AND POTENTIAL OUTCOME SPREAD

- **Card 1:** the current situation
- **Card 2:** blocks or challenges
- **Card 3:** advice
- **Card 4:** action
- **Card 5:** the potential outcome.

TREE OF LIFE SPREAD

- **Card 1, Kether:** higher purpose behind the situation
- **Card 2, Chokmah:** divine wisdom and guidance
- **Card 3, Binah:** current spiritual lessons
- **Card 4, Chesed:** your gifts and talents
- **Card 5, Geburah:** challenges to overcome
- **Card 6, Tipareth:** the heart of the issue
- **Card 7, Netzach:** how to succeed
- **Card 8, Hod:** your current thoughts about the situation
- **Card 9, Yesod:** how to build a strong foundation for your dreams
- **Card 10, Malkuth:** how to bring your desires into manifestation.

Tarot spreads

CELTIC CROSS SPREAD

This spread is based on the original Celtic cross layout with a few slight changes to make it more modern and empowering for present times.

- ✦ **Card 1:** the signifier/you are here
- ✦ **Card 2:** what is influencing or affecting you (this can be a positive influence or a challenge or block)
- ✦ **Card 3:** your subconscious (what you're not seeing or are aware of)
- ✦ **Card 4:** the recent past
- ✦ **Card 5:** the conscious mind (goals, dreams, hopes and so on)
- ✦ **Card 6:** the immediate future if you continue on this path
- ✦ **Card 7:** your heart's desire
- ✦ **Card 8:** advice
- ✦ **Card 9:** action to take
- ✦ **Card 10:** the potential outcome.

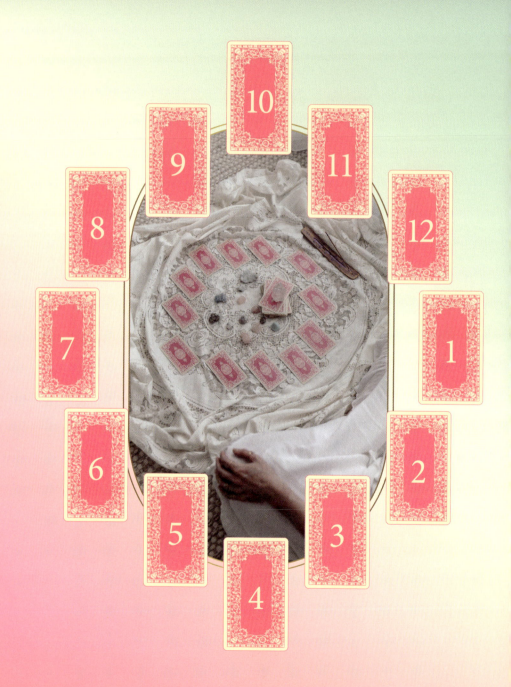

ASTROLOGY SPREAD

This big spread is fantastic to use when you want an overall view of all aspects in your life.

✦ **Card 1, Aries:** the self, the personality, what you are projecting to the world, how others see you
✦ **Card 2, Taurus:** money, the material world
✦ **Card 3, Gemini:** communication, learning, study
✦ **Card 4, Cancer:** home, family
✦ **Card 5, Leo:** love, creativity, fun
✦ **Card 6, Virgo:** details, well-being, everyday aspects of life
✦ **Card 7, Libra:** relationships, balance within the self
✦ **Card 8, Scorpio:** change, transformation, soul growth, shadow work
✦ **Card 9, Sagittarius:** travel, soul searching, beliefs
✦ **Card 10, Capricorn:** career, social status and standing
✦ **Card 11, Aquarius:** social life, hobbies and interests, soul expression
✦ **Card 12, Pisces:** spirituality, subconscious, psychic insights.

THIS OR THAT DECISION SPREAD

If you like you can place a signifier card to represent each choice above each column.

- **Card 1:** positives of option one
- **Card 2:** challenges of option one
- **Card 3:** anything else you need to know about option one
- **Card 4:** positives of option two
- **Card 5:** challenges of option two
- **Card 6:** anything else you need to know about option two
- **Card 7:** how to make the best decision for yourself.

THE FOOL'S
JOURNEY SPREADS

In the following pages you'll find 22 spreads to support and guide you in every phase of your own fool's journey.

The Fool's new beginnings spread

- **Card 1:** the new adventure that awaits
- **Card 2:** fears to face and move through
- **Card 3:** what cannot come on this journey with you
- **Card 4:** what blessings await you
- **Card 5:** how to trust this leap of faith
- **Card 6:** how to land safely.

The Magician's manifestation spread

- **Card 1:** what you think you want or what the ego wants
- **Card 2:** what your heart and soul truly desire
- **Card 3:** how to focus your intention and magic on what you truly desire
- **Card 4:** a ritual to perform to anchor this intention
- **Card 5:** how to energetically become a magnet to attract your intention
- **Card 6:** how to meet the universe halfway
- **Card 7:** how to be open to receiving.

Tarot spreads

The High Priestess's deepening intuition spread

- **Card 1:** how to recognise the voice of your intuition
- **Card 2:** signs you've been seeing
- **Card 3:** guidance you've been receiving
- **Card 4:** inner wisdom you've been avoiding
- **Card 5:** what your intuition is trying to tell you
- **Card 6:** how to develop your intuition
- **Card 7:** how to trust your intuition and yourself.

The Empress's creativity spread

- **Card 1:** where you are at creatively
- **Card 2:** what's affecting or influencing your creativity
- **Card 3:** creative blocks
- **Card 4:** how/where to find inspiration
- **Card 5:** how to find your creative flow
- **Card 6:** how to find time and energy for your creative works
- **Card 7:** how your creativity will benefit you and others.

Tarot spreads

The Emperor's get your shit together spread

- **Card 1:** where your shit is not together
- **Card 2:** what's stopping you from getting it together
- **Card 3:** how to get organised
- **Card 4:** where to focus your energy
- **Card 5:** the best step to take next
- **Card 6:** how to keep your shit together.

The Hierophant's spiritual lessons spread

- **Card 1:** the current challenge or difficulty
- **Card 2:** the spiritual lesson in the challenge
- **Card 3:** how the challenge is helping you grow
- **Card 4:** how to learn the lesson and move forward.

Tarot spreads

The Lovers' romance spread

- **Card 1:** what you need from this relationship
- **Card 2:** what's challenging you in this relationship
- **Card 3:** what your lover needs from you
- **Card 4:** what your lover needs from this relationship
- **Card 5:** what may be challenging your lover
- **Card 6:** what you need to receive from your lover
- **Card 7:** how to make this love work and last.

The Chariot's life purpose direction spread

- **Card 1:** the purpose you've already fulfilled
- **Card 2:** the next phase of your purpose journey
- **Card 3:** challenges to overcome
- **Card 4:** how to get moving in the right direction
- **Card 5:** a short-term goal to work towards
- **Card 6:** how to reach your long-term goals and achieve your purpose.

Tarot spreads

Strength's dealing with difficult times spread

- **Card 1:** the nature of the current challenge
- **Card 2:** how the challenge is affecting you
- **Card 3:** what the challenge is teaching you
- **Card 4:** how to navigate the challenge with courage and strength
- **Card 5:** how to look after yourself and practice self-care in the process.

The Hermit's spiritual development spread

- **Card 1:** spiritual practices that can support you at this time
- **Card 2:** how to find time to retreat and do your inner work
- **Card 3:** how to connect with your inner light
- **Card 4:** inner wisdom to be revealed
- **Card 5:** how to grow and expand your light
- **Card 6:** how your light can light up the world around you.

Wheel of Fortune's luck and success spread

- **Card 1:** limiting beliefs or old stories that hold you back
- **Card 2:** how to release those limiting beliefs now
- **Card 3:** how to live life on your own terms
- **Card 4:** how to activate and embody luck
- **Card 5:** how to activate and embody success
- **Card 6:** how to stay on top.

Justice's finding balance spread

- **Card 1:** where your scales are tipped too far in one direction
- **Card 2:** what's causing this imbalance
- **Card 3:** how to cut and clear this imbalance away
- **Card 4:** how to let go of what's not important
- **Card 5:** how to cultivate deep inner peace, ease and balance
- **Card 6:** how to stay in this balanced state.

Tarot spreads 115

The Hanged Man's spread for when you need to see things differently

- **Card 1:** how did you end up here?
- **Card 2:** what's keeping you stuck and not moving forward?
- **Card 3:** what are you so attached to that it's blocking your path?
- **Card 4:** what do you need to see differently?
- **Card 5:** how to trust and surrender to a different path and outcome.

Death's navigating change and transformation spread

- **Card 1:** what is ending
- **Card 2:** what is changing
- **Card 3:** how this change is challenging you
- **Card 4:** how this change is serving and supporting you
- **Card 5:** where to find help and support
- **Card 6:** new doors that are opening for you
- **Card 7:** what you need to know as you move into this new chapter.

Temperance's inner peace and harmony spread

- **Card 1:** what is preventing your peace
- **Card 2:** what is harshing your harmony
- **Card 3:** how to come back into balance within yourself
- **Card 4:** how to create more balance in your environment
- **Card 5:** how to find more peace in your relationships
- **Card 6:** how to find harmony within your soul.

The Devil's break the chains spread

- **Card 1:** what limiting thoughts and beliefs are holding you back
- **Card 2:** how your choices and actions are keeping you stuck
- **Card 3:** who/what is controlling you
- **Card 4:** how to release blame
- **Card 5:** how to realise you are not the victim; you are the victor!
- **Card 6:** how to break the chains and free yourself.

Tarot spreads

The Tower's releasing and letting go spread

✦ **Card 1:** what thoughts and beliefs no longer work for you

✦ **Card 2:** what ways of being and acting are now outdated

✦ **Card 3:** what else is no longer working in your life

✦ **Card 4:** the potential outcome if you don't let go

✦ **Card 5:** how to trust and let go of what you've built that no longer works

✦ **Card 6:** how to rebuild in a better way.

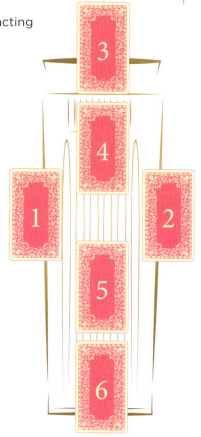

The Star's divine light and wisdom spread

- **Card 1:** how to see your light and radiance
- **Card 2:** how to connect with higher divine wisdom
- **Card 3:** a message of divine inspiration
- **Card 4:** a message of hope
- **Card 5:** a message from the highest divine wisdom
- **Card 6:** how to stay shiny
- **Card 7:** how to stay connected with the higher realms of light.

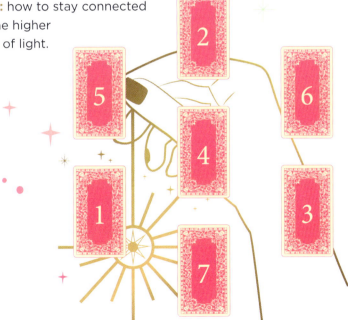

The Moon's navigating the unknown spread

- **Card 1:** how to access your inner light in the darkness
- **Card 2:** illusions to cast light upon
- **Card 3:** one small step to take
- **Card 4:** how to trust yourself and your guides when you can't see the path
- **Card 5:** who/what is guiding you safely through the unknown
- **Card 6:** how to follow the light of your heart in the darkness.

The Sun's path to joy and happiness spread

- ✦ **Card 1:** what brings you joy
- ✦ **Card 2:** what blocks your joy
- ✦ **Card 3:** how to shine light on the blocks and dissolve them
- ✦ **Card 4:** how to become excited about life again
- ✦ **Card 5:** the blessings that more happiness and joy will bring to your life
- ✦ **Card 6:** how to share your blessings and bring more joy and happiness to the world.

Judgement's clearing and healing karma spread

- **Card 1:** old baggage you are holding on to
- **Card 2:** how holding old baggage is creating problems for you
- **Card 3:** how to release old baggage now
- **Card 4:** what needs healing from the past
- **Card 5:** how to heal the past now
- **Card 6:** how to forgive and heal yourself and move on
- **Card 7:** how to create good karma moving forward.

The World's wish fulfilment spread

- **Card 1:** your wish (you can choose this card upright if you want to)
- **Card 2:** a ritual or spell to perform to anchor your intention
- **Card 3:** how to strengthen your belief that this wish will come true
- **Card 4:** action to take
- **Card 5:** how to stay open to receiving your wish
- **Card 6:** how to celebrate when your wish comes true
- **Card 7:** how to move forward on the path of even more wish fulfilment.

Tarot spreads

THE WANDS' PASSION AND PURPOSE SPREAD

- **Card 1:** your passion
- **Card 2:** your purpose
- **Card 3:** how to take action and make this happen
- **Card 4:** the potential outcome.

THE CUPS' HEART-OPENING SPREAD

- **Card 1:** how to love yourself more deeply
- **Card 2:** how to have more compassion for yourself
- **Card 3:** how to have more compassion for others
- **Card 4:** how to open your heart to more blessings and all good things.

THE SWORDS' POSITIVE MINDSET SPREAD

- **Card 1:** how your current mindset is affecting you
- **Card 2:** how to cut through mental blocks and negative patterns
- **Card 3:** how to create a positive mindset moving forward
- **Card 4:** how a more positive mindset can change your life.

THE PENTACLES' PROSPERITY SPREAD

- **Card 1:** the current situation with prosperity
- **Card 2:** blocks to receiving and creating more prosperity
- **Card 3:** how to release the blocks and create a flow of abundance
- **Card 4:** how to create an overflow of prosperity.

Tarot spreads

EXPANDED CARD MEANINGS

You can use the expanded card meanings in whatever way you wish. For a deeper understanding of the cards you can read this section front to back, noticing the journey that you're taken on from the moment The Fool steps out onto the cliff's edge to the mastery achieved by the King of Pentacles, or you can simply use this section as a reference for when you're doing your own readings.

INQUIRY QUESTIONS

Each card meaning includes two inquiry questions to help you use your readings to make positive change in your life. You can use these questions:

✦ for considering and thinking

✦ to deeply meditate on

✦ as journal prompts

✦ to expand your reading by pulling a tarot card for each question.

RITUALS

The rituals included as part of each card meaning can be used as a magical practice to help you activate, integrate or move through the energy, lessons, blessings and wisdom of the cards that you feel most drawn to, those that keep showing up in readings or that you find challenging in your readings.

TRUSTING YOUR INTUITION

Before you look at the meanings in the book ask these questions:

✦ What's the first thing you notice about this card: does something in the image grab your attention?

✦ Do any words, phrases or song lyrics come to mind?

✦ How do you feel about this card?

✦ What does this card make you think of?

A NOTE ON CORRESPONDENCES

Planetary and zodiacal: there are various methods of aligning planets and zodiac signs with the tarot. Those included in this book are based on the original Rider-Waite-Smith correspondences.

Crystals, herbs and oils: the correspondences for crystals, herbs and oils in this section are inspired by various systems and paths including Wicca, witchcraft, ceremonial magic and my own intuition. If a card inspires you and you want to embody and attract that energy these tools can support you in doing that. If you're experiencing a difficult time and seeing that reflected in some of the more challenging cards of the tarot, these tools can support you in navigating through this time with more ease.

If you don't have the tools mentioned in this book you can always use what you have: you never have to buy anything or have the most expensive crystal or oil. See page 82 for some information on general all-purpose tools and pages 82 and 83 for more information on how to work with crystals, herbs and oils.

Tarot time!

Separate the 22 major arcana cards from your deck and place them face up in order. Look at the major arcana and think about which cards represent different points in your own journey so far. When were you The Fool off on a new adventure? When were you The Emperor, grounded and in control of your life? When were you The Hermit, needing time out from the world? Go through the 22 majors and see your own story reflected in the cards.

Find a card that you feel represents what you are going through right now and journal on these questions:

✦ What aspect or situation in your life do you see reflected in this card?
✦ How does this card make you feel?
✦ How does it feel knowing this is something everyone experiences on their journey?
✦ Pull a card and ask: 'How can I navigate through this to the outcome I most desire?'

THE FOOL'S JOURNEY

It is time to take your journey with, or rather *as*, The Fool. The 22 cards of the major arcana tell the story of The Fool's journey and reflect on the steps, experiences and ups and downs of your own life and spiritual journey.

0. THE FOOL

Beginnings, leaps of faith, innocence, trust, free spirit, freedom, taking risks or chances, naiveté, spontaneity, adventure, worry free, enthusiasm, silliness, light-hearted, joker, fearless, optimistic, hopeful, travel, leaving home, start of a new adventure or phase of life, clean slate, new cycle, trust, faith, dawn

Correspondences
- Celestial body/sign: Uranus
- Element: air
- Crystal: clear quartz
- Herb: cedar
- Oil: lemon

Imagery: With nothing to weigh him down but just a few possessions in his bag and a small dog representing loyalty and protection on his heels, The Fool stands on the edge of a cliff, completely unaware that he is about to step off into the great unknown.

Empowering meanings
- A new adventure or a new way of being is calling. There is a great potential for positive change. The slate is wiped clear, there is nothing to hold onto from the past: only the bright future ahead of you to look towards.
- See the world with child-like wonder. Reconnect with your inner free spirit.

- Have a beginner's mind. No matter how much you think you know or how much experience you have, there is always so much more to discover on the journey.
- Let go of attachment to outcomes. Trust that you will be guided and that all will be well.
- Take leaps of faith. Take chances. You only live this life once, so make the most of it!

Reversed meanings: Foolishness or recklessness, a need to pause before jumping in, resistance to starting something new, not paying attention to what's in front of you, being overly cautious.

Inquiry questions
- What is the leap I'm being called to take?
- How can I be more free-spirited?

Affirmations
- I trust my journey.
- I trust that the universe will always guide me and catch me if I fall.

Ritual: Go outside (or visualise) and lift your face towards the sun. Feel the rays lightening your heart and spirit.

1. THE MAGICIAN

Power, magic, ritual, manifestation, focused energy, skill, control, willpower, inspiration, charisma, intention, potential, magical talents, personal power, magnetism, harnessing or controlling energy, connecting the spiritual and material, magical or ritual tools, the elements, resources, having everything you need at your disposal, taking aligned action

Correspondences
- Celestial body/sign: Mercury
- Element: air
- Crystal: fire opal
- Herb: star anise
- Oil: lavender

Imagery: The Magician stands behind an altar on which sit his magical tools: a wand, cup, sword and pentacle, representing the four elements and the suits of the tarot. He has everything he needs to create the outcome he desires. The Magician holds a wand in the air with one hand while pointing at the earth with the other, signifying his connection with both the spiritual and material worlds. He is surrounded by roses (love, the soul and wisdom) and lilies (purity, transformation, spirituality and compassion).

Empowering meanings
- You have the power. You have everything you need to succeed.

- Your dreams, goals and desires are within reach as long as you stay in your power and keep your energy and intention focused in the right direction.
- You may need to develop or draw on reserves of willpower.
- Take action and meet the universe halfway and you may be amazed at what you can create and achieve!
- The power is in your hands, so use it wisely.

Reversed meanings: A disconnection from, resistance to or even fear of your own power, not taking responsibility for your own life. Not seeing or using the resources you have at your disposal. Manipulation or misuse of power.

Inquiry questions
- Where is my power in this situation?
- What tools, skills or experience do I have that can help me overcome my current challenges and manifest my desires?

Affirmations
- I have the power!
- I have everything I need to succeed!

Ritual: Create an altar that includes something to represent each of the elements.

2. THE HIGH PRIESTESS

Intuition, divine feminine, mysteries, secrets, inner knowing, the goddess, cycles, the spiritual veil, hidden aspects, the unconscious, psychic insights, the occult, dreams, seeking counsel

Correspondences
- ✦ Celestial body/sign: moon
- ✦ Element: water
- ✦ Crystal: moonstone
- ✦ Herb: jasmine
- ✦ Oil: clary sage

Imagery: The High Priestess sits between the two pillars, one dark and one light, symbolising harmony in duality. She wears robes and a crown of thorns, symbolising her connection with the moon's phases and divine feminine wisdom. The crescent moon at her feet symbolises a deep grounding in and trust of her own intuition. She holds the Torah (wisdom) and sits in front of a veil of pomegranates, representing abundance, the divine feminine and spiritual attainment and enlightenment and the spiritual veil that you begin to see through as you journey on the spiritual path.

Empowering meanings
- ✦ The answers are already within you. Trust your own intuition.
- ✦ If you have a sense about a decision you need to make or course of action to take, trust that inner knowing. Trust yourself.

- ✦ Seek out the answers if you feel called, or simply trust that all will be revealed in time.

- ✦ Spiritual or divine mysteries, truths and teachings will be revealed to you when you are ready to receive them.

- ✦ The High Priestess is a powerful guide for tarot readers and those exploring spiritual and occult mysteries. She may not immediately give you all the answers you seek, but when she shows up you can be sure you are on the right path.

Reversed meanings: Ignoring or not trusting your own intuition, forcing a spiritual experience or connection, being impatient with divine guidance or timing. Potential to push for answers and information that may not be in your best interest to have at this time.

Inquiry questions
- ✦ What is my intuition telling me?
- ✦ How can I trust myself and my inner guidance?

Affirmations
- ✦ I always have access to my own inner knowing.
- ✦ I trust my intuition.

Ritual: Check the phase and sign that the moon is in right now and use this as extra guidance.

3. THE EMPRESS

Creativity, nurture, Divine Mother, fertility, abundance, beauty, connection with the natural world, conception, gratitude, motherhood, raising or teaching children, sensuality, satisfaction, grounding, health and well-being, divine feminine flow

Correspondences
- Celestial body/sign: Venus
- Element: earth
- Crystal: chrysocolla
- Herb: rose
- Oil: ylang ylang

Imagery: The Empress sits on a comfy throne surrounded by symbols of abundance: a lush forest and a field of wheat. Her crown of 12 stars represents the cycles of time and her robe is decorated in pomegranates, representing the divine feminine and abundance. A heart-shaped shield with the symbol of Venus sits at her feet and she holds a sceptre with a round globe on top, showing us that she is a good and heart-centred leader. The waterfall symbolises nourishment and divine feminine flow.

Empowering meanings
- Nourish and nurture your own mind, body and spirit, dreams, goals and creative projects. Look after, love and cherish those close to you.

- ✦ If you've been sitting on something that's ready to be birthed into the world, this may be the time to do it.

- ✦ While you are in gratitude for all the abundance and love already in your life, this is also a good time to plant seeds and set intentions. Don't forget to keep watering and caring for these seeds as they grow.

- ✦ Move into a divine feminine flow. Let things come to you: don't chase, attract.

- ✦ Your relationship with your own mother, mother figures, children or those you look after in any way may need your focus.

Reversed meanings: Difficulties or resistance towards looking after yourself and/or others, inability to see your abundance, overly protective of creative projects. Potential issues in relationships with your mother or mother figures or in your role as a mother or nurturer.

Inquiry questions
- ✦ How can I mother and nurture myself?
- ✦ How can I give birth to my dreams?

Affirmations
- ✦ I am creative and abundant.
- ✦ I nourish and nurture myself.

Ritual: Pick or buy some flowers for yourself.

4. THE EMPEROR

Leadership, order, divine masculine, organisation, rules, structure, stability, wisdom, discipline, power, strength, boundaries, control, routine, self-control, authority, ambition, protection, conviction

Correspondences
- Celestial body/sign: Aries
- Element: fire
- Crystal: red jasper
- Herb: basil
- Oil: cedarwood

Imagery: The Emperor sits on his throne of ram heads representing the sign of Aries. He wears a gold crown and red robes, symbolising the masculine energy of Mars. His armour tells us he has just returned from or is heading into battle. His long white beard is symbolic of his years of wisdom and experience. He holds an ankh sceptre in one hand, the ancient Egyptian symbol for everlasting life, and a globe in the other, a symbol of the kingdom that he rules over.

Empowering meanings
- It's time to get organised, disciplined and focused. Structure and routine will help you achieve your goals.
- If you want something to change within yourself or within your life, you are the one who has to make that happen.

- You may be called into a leadership position or asked to take the lead in some way. Others look up to and rely on you for wisdom, guidance and direction. Be a guiding light for others.
- Relationships with your father, father figures, bosses or authority figures are highlighted here.

Reversed meanings: Difficult relationships with father figures or bosses, too much or not enough discipline and structure, being overbearing or undermining, resistance to self-discipline and organisation.

Inquiry questions
- How could more discipline and organisation help me right now?
- Which rules need following? Which ones need breaking and recreating?

Affirmations
- I am safe and I am stable.
- I inspire others with my strength, wisdom and courage.

Ritual: Tidy your desk or workspace.

5. THE HIEROPHANT

Spiritual teacher, advice, tradition, mentor, respect, spiritual community or institution, seeking counsel, sacredness, channelling, a prophet, spiritual discipline, giving and receiving spiritual teachings and/or wisdom

Correspondences
- Celestial body/sign: Taurus
- Element: earth
- Crystal: lapis lazuli
- Herb: sage
- Oil: frankincense

Imagery: The Hierophant has the appearance of a pope giving a sermon to his congregation of two. He is dressed in religious garments, a tall hat, which is symbolic of his connection with the divine, and holds a triple or papal cross showing his high status. He holds his hand in a symbol of blessing or sign that he is speaking or teaching. He sits between two pillars with the keys of heaven at his feet.

The traditional imagery for The Hierophant can be confronting to those who have a negative association with the church, but when upright he can represent a wise spiritual teacher of any tradition or path.

Empowering meanings
- Seek advice from a spiritual teacher or someone you trust and respect who is wise and experienced in the matter at hand.

- Always receive the advice of others with discernment and trust your intuition, but sometimes guidance or confirmation from a trusted source is also needed.
- Seek out spiritual teachings and look to spiritual paths and practices that have stood the test of time. Be open to learning from those who have come before. At the same time, be aware of and avoid dogmatic teachings that make no room for questioning or evolution.

Reversed meanings: Spiritual teachers without integrity, spiritual teachings that are outdated or problematic, spiritual groups that have lost their way, resistance to or pushing back from tradition.

Inquiry questions
- What traditions are worth keeping?
- What traditions are outdated and no longer serve and support me?

Affirmations
- I have respect for and uphold the traditions that are important to me.
- I let go of outdated traditions and create new ones.

Ritual: Listen to an audio book or talk by a spiritual teacher you respect.

6. THE LOVERS

Love, romance, self-love, divine love, true love, passion, communication, harmony, heart-centred decision, divine union of souls, commitment, devotion, duality, choices, two opposites coming together

Correspondences
- Celestial body/sign: Gemini
- Element: air
- Crystal: rose quartz
- Herb: damiana
- Oil: rose

Imagery: A man and a woman stand naked beneath Archangel Raphael, who appears from a cloud. Behind the woman is the apple tree from the garden of Eden. The serpent is a symbol of temptation but also of knowledge and power. The 12 flames of the tree behind the man symbolise passion and desire, the zodiac signs and the cycles of time. The volcano behind them threatens to erupt in uncontrolled passion.

Empowering meanings
- Things are looking good in the areas of love and romance, but there is a deeper meaning here. A higher love is available to you now and you may be feeling or working towards deeper self-love, self-realisation, inner harmony, balance and peace or a deeper spiritual and devotional relationship with the divine.

- You always have a choice when it comes to love. When kindred spirits enter your life, you have free will and can choose how to move forward in relationships.
- There is a gentle warning here not to let sexual passion or lust rule your decision-making in matters of the heart or anywhere in your life.
- Focus on experiencing deeper love and connection with others and yourself and within all aspects of your life.

Reversed meanings: A challenging relationship, difficulties in love and romance, disconnection from the divine, lack of self-love, making decisions out of passion or lust over love.

Inquiry questions
- How can I experience deeper love for myself and my life?
- Where am I letting passion rather than love control my actions?

Affirmations
- I am loved.
- My relationships are positive and harmonious.

Ritual: Look in the mirror and tell yourself 'I love you.'

7. THE CHARIOT

Forward momentum, overcoming obstacles, determination, drive, self-control, willpower, victory, success, trials of initiation, conquest, travel, mastery, triumph, taking the reins, clear direction

Correspondences
- Celestial body/sign: Cancer
- Element: water
- Crystal: carnelian
- Herb: lemongrass
- Oil: eucalyptus

Imagery: The charioteer holds up a wand, symbolising his ability to direct his intention and manifest it into the material world. Above him is a canopy of stars and at the helm are two sphinxes, symbolising spiritual mysteries. One sphinx is black and the other one white, symbolising duality. The winged disc sits at the front of his chariot and the lingam and yoni symbols sit beneath it, representing the merging of and balance of two opposing forces. The city sits behind him, showing that he's on the road and moving forward.

Empowering meanings
- Things can and will move ahead. Obstacles can be overcome.
- Strength, determination, drive and will can get you where you want to go.

- Plan for the journey: get clear on your direction and get your mind and intention aligned and into balance and harmony for a fast and easy journey.
- The road ahead is open. Whether you are travelling by land, sea, air or taking an inner spiritual journey you will reach your destination.
- Stay in your power, stay in the driver's seat and stay aligned with your goal.

Reversed meanings: Blocks in the road, difficulties getting going, letting obstacles defeat you, a resistance to being in the driver's seat of your own life. Potential for spinning your wheels or going around in circles.

Inquiry questions
- Am I going in the right direction?
- How can I develop the willpower I need to steer my own chariot?

Affirmations
- All roads are open and clear.
- I move forward now towards victory and success!

Ritual: Draw a black wing on the bottom of your right shoe and a white wing on your left shoe.

8. STRENGTH

Courage, bravery, vulnerability, courageous heart, confidence, courage to face your challenges head on, perseverance, compassion, patience, mastering emotions, mastering the mind, inner power, self-control, serenity, integrity, being true to yourself, self-esteem

Correspondences
- Celestial body/sign: Leo
- Element: fire
- Crystal: tiger's eye
- Herb: sunflower
- Oil: ginger

Imagery: A woman dressed in white gently opens the mouth of a fierce lion, representing the fierce, animalistic part of your own nature. She wears a crown of roses, symbols of abundance, love and wisdom. A symbol of eternity sits above her head, reminding you of the continuation of all things.

Empowering meanings
- True strength is not in how physically strong you are but in vulnerability, in being true to who you are and living with a courageous heart. Your strength is found when you anchor more deeply into love and compassion, stand up for what you believe in and choose to live by your own moral code.

- ✦ You have the strength and power to overcome any challenges in your life as long as you work on mastering your emotions and mind.
- ✦ Live a big, bold life, be strong and proud of who you are and live with your heart open wide.
- ✦ Share your heart, vulnerabilities, truth, passions and light with the world. As you activate your inner power you will inspire so many others to do the same.
- ✦ Whatever you are going through you will get through it, with love and courage.

Reversed meanings: A closed heart, lacking courage to be true to yourself, fear of being vulnerable or seen as weak. Giving in or giving up, showing strength through aggression and hostility.

Inquiry questions
- ✦ What are my strengths?
- ✦ How can I live with a courageous heart?

Affirmations
- ✦ I have the strength to overcome any challenge or obstacle.
- ✦ I have the courage to live a big, bold and heart-centred life.

Ritual: Create a simple sigil or symbol to represent a lion. Draw it on yourself using oil, eyeliner or a visualisation of light when you need courage.

Expanded card meanings

9. THE HERMIT

Retreat, meditation, inner light, going within, rest, relaxation, contemplation, reflection, a spiritual teacher, spirit guide, the higher self, spiritual pilgrimage, spiritual journey, inner work, introspection, maturity, reflection, finding yourself

Correspondences

- Celestial body/sign: Virgo
- Element: earth
- Crystal: peridot
- Herb: myrrh
- Oil: patchouli

Imagery: An old man dressed in robes holds a lantern in one hand and a tall stick in the other as he stands in the darkness. His hood is covering his head as he looks down, showing us that he is more concerned with his inner journey than what is happening around him. He has retreated into his own space and inner world.

Empowering meanings

- Disconnect to reconnect. Spend time alone in quiet meditation and reflection as an antidote to burnout and the stresses of modern life.
- Take time to connect with your heart, mind and inner light away from the noise, thoughts, opinions and ideas of others in order to find yourself again.

- As you take this time out you may experience deep spiritual revelations and receive the guidance you've been asking for and you will emerge well rested and recharged, ready to again shine your light out into the world.
- This is not a time to take action, but rather to contemplate your journey so far and your choices and path.
- The Hermit can also signify a deeply spiritual person who may be you!

Reversed meanings: Resistance to rest, doing too much, energetic burnout. Potential for too much solitude or loneliness and the need to come back out of retreat and rejoin the world.

Inquiry questions
- How can I find time and space to rest and retreat?
- What guidance does my inner light and wisdom have for me?

Affirmations
- I am more effective in the world when I take time to rest and recharge.
- My inner work is just as important as how I show up in the world.

Ritual: Take a social media break or turn off your phone. Do this for a few hours, days or weeks.

Expanded card meanings

155

10. WHEEL OF FORTUNE

Luck, fortune, destiny, success, positive change, opportunities, cosmic momentum, cycles, karma, chance, expansion, direction, movement, what goes around comes around

Correspondences

- Celestial body/sign: Jupiter
- Element: fire
- Crystal: gold rutile quartz
- Herb: cinnamon
- Oil: clove

Imagery: A wheel hovers in the sky surrounded by clouds and winged figures. A sphinx, symbolising spiritual mysteries, wisdom and the soul, sits on top holding a sword while Anubis, the god of the underworld, holds the wheel up from beneath. A serpent, representing knowledge, wisdom and temptation, slithers along the side. On the wheel is the Tetragrammaton or the name of God, YHVH, and the letters ROTA, which mean 'wheel' in Latin. Also present are the alchemical symbols for Mercury, sulphur, water and salt, the building blocks of life. The four fixed signs of the zodiac are symbolised by the winged beings in each corner: the man for Aquarius, the eagle for Scorpio, the lion for Leo and the bull for Taurus.

Empowering meanings

✦ Fate is on your side. Destiny is calling. Things are turning out in your favour!

✦ If things have been feeling tough for a while, this is a sign that you will soon come out of any difficulties and be back on top again.

✦ This is a card of destiny: trust that you are on the right path and that all that is meant for you will find you, as you long as you keep your heart, mind and eyes open.

✦ Be present to all the blessings in your life and stay positive, and you will find you are able to stay on top of the wheel more often than not.

✦ You can create your own fate and make your own luck in this life.

Reversed meanings: Times of difficulty or struggle, things feeling like they are not turning out in your favour or going to plan, resistance to your destiny.

Inquiry questions

✦ What is going well for me right now?

✦ When life gets me down, how can I get back up again?

Affirmations

✦ Everything turns out in my favour.

✦ Good things are happening for me.

Ritual: Hold a coin in your hand and affirm this is your lucky coin. Carry it with you as a lucky talisman.

Expanded card meanings

11. JUSTICE

Truth, balance, integrity, fairness, accountability, honesty, doing what's right, legal issues, karma, retribution, judgement, ethics, morals, law, ethical decision-making

Correspondences
- Celestial body/sign: Libra
- Element: air
- Crystal: blue lace agate
- Herb: calendula
- Oil: geranium

Imagery: A judge in a crown and robes sits between two pillars, representing balance and harmony between opposing forces. The judge holds a sword of truth in one hand and a set of balanced scales, symbolising balance and fairness, in the other. A veil sits behind the judge, representing compassion in making decisions.

Empowering meanings
- Justice will prevail.
- Trust in the law of karma, knowing that eventually everyone will stand before Justice's sword and scales, including you.
- Look at your life and consider the effects of your actions. Focus on creating positive karma for yourself and living your life with integrity, truth and doing the right thing so you reap positive karmic rewards.

- Consider how your actions and choices are affecting others and your future self, either positively or negatively.
- Justice can also represent legal issues or court cases.

Reversed meanings: Not being held to account, unfair punishment, difficulties within the legal system, dishonesty, unfairness, creating negative karma.

Inquiry questions
- How can I be just, fair and honest in all my dealings?
- How can I live with more integrity and balance?

Affirmations
- I make balanced and aligned decisions.
- I am fair and honest, and I live a life of integrity.

Ritual: Do a good deed to balance your karma.

Expanded card meanings

159

12. THE HANGED MAN

Patience, perspective, surrender, stuck, stagnant, blocked, hung up, strung out, waiting, pause, realisation, awakening, understanding, freeing yourself, listening to inner wisdom, unconventional thinking or behaviour, self-sacrifice, breakthrough

Correspondences

- ✦ Celestial body/sign: Neptune
- ✦ Element: water
- ✦ Crystal: beryl
- ✦ Herb: willow
- ✦ Oil: ambergris

Imagery: A figure hangs upside down with one foot tied to a tree. Although his hands are bound behind him and he's in an uncomfortable position, The Hanged Man is not struggling and his expression is calm and relaxed. A golden halo surrounds his head, indicating a spiritual epiphany or realisation.

Empowering meanings

- ✦ Have patience. Things may feel stuck or stagnant right now, but the way out and through is via trusting and surrendering to the process and looking at things from a different perspective.
- ✦ You may not be able to control what's happening in your life right now, but you can change your thoughts and how you feel about it.

- ✦ Struggling, fighting and resistance will keep you stuck.
- ✦ There is a lesson to learn here, and once you've learned it you will be able to move forward again.
- ✦ Meditate and be open to spiritual guidance and wisdom, realisation and inspiration.
- ✦ The Hanged Man can also appear when it's time to cut negative cords of attachment with others.

Reversed meanings: You may not be seeing the situation clearly or are still hanging on to something that is ready to be released. When reversed this card can indicate you are now free from the ties that bind you.

Inquiry questions
- ✦ What do I need to see differently in this situation?
- ✦ Where am I creating knots within myself and my life?

Affirmations
- ✦ I'm open to seeing things from different perspectives.
- ✦ I trust and surrender.

Ritual: Tie a piece of cotton around a candle. When the candle burns down and breaks the cord, know that any stuck energy has been cleared.

Expanded card meanings

161

13. DEATH

Change, transformation, thresholds, portals, endings and beginnings, doors closing and windows opening, natural cycles of life and time, moving into a new state of being, renewal, liberation, out with the old in with the new

Correspondences

- Celestial body/sign: Scorpio
- Element: water
- Crystal: obsidian
- Herb: blackthorn
- Oil: cypress

Imagery: Death in the form of a skeletal figure rides a white horse, a symbol of purity, while figures lie on the ground nearby or plead with him as he passes. Waving a black flag featuring a white rose, another symbol of purification, beauty and rebirth, this vision of death certainly projects an intimidating picture. However, off in the distance a sun begins to rise, reminding you that death is not the end but rather a transition to the next place.

Empowering meanings

- This is a powerful time of change and transformation. Something is ending or needs to end so you can move into the next chapter of your life.
- This change may come in the form of something in your life – a job loss, end of a relationship or a house move – or it

can be an inner change, a shift in your energy, state of mind or consciousness.

✦ Whatever is ending in your life will be replaced by something new. This is a promise that that there is always light at the end of what sometimes feels like a very dark tunnel.

✦ This card can also represent grief and the grieving process: grieving for passed-over loved ones, things that didn't work out, dreams that were not fulfilled or unlived lives. Give yourself permission to grieve and seek out support if it's needed.

Reversed meanings: Fear of change, loss, letting go or moving on, staying stuck in situations that no longer serve you, struggling with the grieving process.

Inquiry questions
✦ What has come to its completion?
✦ How can I let go of the past so I can move into my future?

Affirmations
✦ I release and let go of the past.
✦ I am transforming into a more radiant version of myself.

Ritual: Write down what you need to let go of and then bury the paper, laying it to rest.

Expanded card meanings

14. TEMPERANCE

Harmony, moderation, right action, balance, alignment, peace, calm, mediator, release of ego, taking the middle path, not taking sides, healing, self-control, resolution, optimism, blending or combining of beliefs or ideas, angelic beings

Correspondences
- Celestial body/sign: Sagittarius
- Element: fire
- Crystal: amethyst
- Herb: angelica
- Oil: angelica

Imagery: An angel stands with one foot in calm water and one on the earth, symbolic of the balance between the elements and the spiritual and material. The angel pours water from two cups into each other, blending and balancing these opposite forces. The triangle in a square on the angel's tunic represents the balance between body, mind and spirit. The path and sun in the background represent the journey of life.

Empowering meanings
- Harmony and balance are needed right now. Wherever you are leaning too much in one direction, bring yourself back into alignment.
- You may be working too hard and not resting enough, being too harsh on yourself and not showing yourself enough

compassion, focused too much on the material aspects of life and not enough on the spiritual.

✦ Focusing on inner balance will help you deal with whatever life brings you in a more effective, calm and mature way.

✦ If you are trying to make a decision, you are being called to take right action. Avoid doing what is easy or will boost your ego, but instead do what is right for you and all involved.

✦ Avoid taking sides and be the mediator, with others and with yourself.

Reversed meanings: Feeling out of balance or alignment, struggling to find inner peace, taking sides or being too extreme in your thinking or actions.

Inquiry questions
✦ How can I find more inner peace and balance?
✦ How can I walk the middle path?

Affirmations
✦ I am balanced and aligned.
✦ I am in harmony with myself and others.

Ritual: Visualise that you are a pillar of light and are centred and aligned.

Expanded card meanings

165

15. THE DEVIL

The shadow, the material, breaking the chains, feeling trapped or stuck, control, limitations, boundaries, sexual desires, instant gratification, confronting inner demons, overindulgence, red flags, fear, obsession, temptation, addiction, materialism

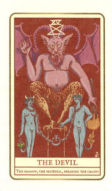

Correspondences

- Celestial body/sign: Capricorn
- Element: earth
- Crystal: aragonite
- Herb: black pepper
- Oil: vetiver

Imagery: A devil sits in darkness as he lords over a naked couple in chains. The Devil wears a reversed pentagram on his forehead. When upright this is a symbol of balance and harmony within all the elements, goodness, magic, life and protection. When reversed the symbol places spirit at the bottom and earth at the top, representing a focus on the material rather than the spiritual.

The Christian concept of The Devil was originally created by the church out of a distorted image of the pagan horned god Pan, in part to make paganism seem like the devil's work to control the population and their congregation through fear. While this imagery can be unsettling, it is nothing more than an ancient attempt at control and manipulation.

Empowering meanings

✦ You may be feeling trapped or stuck or as though you're being controlled by something outside of you: someone difficult in your life, a situation you can't control or your inner demons, fears or negative thought patterns.

✦ There could be too much focus on the material world and not enough on the spiritual and higher self.

✦ Deep dive into some shadow work. Look at your fears, habits and difficult truths about yourself, then bring these to light to be seen, released and healed. Love yourself through the process.

✦ Whether you are trapped by your own thoughts, beliefs or stories you've been telling yourself or by a situation you feel you have no power over, know that you do have the power to break the chains and free yourself.

✦ Temptation or addiction may be highlighted here. Look at what you struggle to have control over such as substances, food, social media and so on and consider how you can take back control or get professional support if it's needed.

✦ If The Devil appears when asking about a person, stay in your power and discernment.

Reversed meanings: Chains being broken, freedom, release, a realisation of your power or taking back your power. Potential inability to see or work with your shadow aspects effectively or unable to escape and break the chains yourself. If this is the case, seek support.

Expanded card meanings

167

Inquiry questions

✦ What is holding me back?

✦ What unhelpful stories am I telling myself?

Affirmations

✦ I call all my power back to me.

✦ I break the chains and free myself.

Ritual: Take a piece of string and tie knots in it to represent your fears and challenges. Cut or burn the string to symbolise these chains being broken.

16. THE TOWER

Divine intervention, sudden change, epiphany, realisation, enlightenment, a shake-up, destruction and rebuilding, removal of illusion, spiritual awakening, changing your life, the unexpected, outdated beliefs, ideas or opinions, opportunity for change, opportunity for growth, liberation, purification, release, letting go

Correspondences

- ✦ Celestial body/sign: Mars
- ✦ Element: fire
- ✦ Crystal: smoky quartz
- ✦ Herb: garlic
- ✦ Oil: tea tree

Imagery: The divine light hits the tower in a lightning bolt of realisation, shaking up the people inside. They tumble to the ground, unable to stay within the old, outdated structure they have created for themselves. Golden yods fall around the tower, a symbol of the divine.

Empowering meanings

- ✦ This is an invitation to make much-needed change in your life, with no option to RSVP. If you don't make these changes the universe may take the situation out of your hands and make it happen for you. An example of the tower at work is getting guidance to leave your current job, ignoring it and getting fired but then finding a much better work situation more in alignment with your soul.

✦ For those on a spiritual journey, path of self-development, ascension or enlightenment: rejoice! You have another opportunity to see new truths, remove another veil of illusion and gain deeper personal and spiritual wisdom and insight.

✦ You may feel some discomfort when The Tower appears, but this may be exactly what you need in order to grow, evolve and vibrate higher. You have the opportunity to release what no longer serves, let go of the old and rebuild something so much stronger and better.

Reversed meanings: Resistance to change, fighting against divine intervention, refusing to listen to your intuition or guidance, staying in a place, situation or mindset that no longer serves you. Potential to struggle to rebuild after a challenging time.

Inquiry questions
✦ What illusions are being shattered?
✦ What do I know I need to change in my life?

Affirmations
✦ I am willing to let go of what no longer serves me.
✦ I take action on divine guidance.

Ritual: Draw a lightning bolt on a piece of paper and write around it everything you are ready to hand over to divine intervention. Burn, bury or recycle the piece of paper.

17. THE STAR

Inspiration, hope, divine wisdom, divine connection, higher self, optimism, spiritual development, possibilities, blessings, shining your light, regeneration, renewal, nature-based spirituality, peace, serenity, bright promises, spirit guides, star beings, tranquillity, nonconformity, faith, soul star chakra

Correspondences

- Celestial body/sign: Aquarius
- Element: air
- Crystal: aquamarine
- Herb: chamomile
- Oil: melissa

Imagery: A bright yellow star appears in the night sky, surrounded by seven smaller white ones. Each has eight sides, representing infinity or eternity. A woman kneels under the stars pouring one pot into the pond and one onto the earth, showing that she nourishes both the spiritual and the physical. A bird sits on a tree in the background, representing the elements of air and spirit and the beings of divine light who guide you.

Empowering meanings

- Stay hopeful and look on the bright side of life. Look to the stars, follow the sparks of divine inspiration. Listen to your inner wisdom and connect with spirit and your spiritual self.

- There is a bigger picture, a higher plan, and you have the power to access it through trusting, following and shining your inner light.
- Try to stay optimistic and hopeful about life, even in the face of difficulties. It is that hope and connection with higher powers that will get you through this life.
- If you've lost hope, The Star is here to remind you that life is still beautiful.
- Have faith, trusting that everything is working out. Anchor into your spiritual beliefs and practices to support you.
- Have hope that everything will work out in the highest ways for you now and always.

Reversed meanings: Disconnection from the spiritual, inability to see or accept deeper spiritual truths, lack of inspiration, feeling hopeless, lack of belief in yourself, being closed to the wonder and beauty of life and the universe.

Inquiry questions
- How can I connect with the divine light and love of the universe?
- How can I feel hopeful about my future?

Affirmations
- I am hopeful and optimistic about my life.
- Things are looking up!

Ritual: Look up at the stars and reconnect with the magic of the universe.

Expanded card meanings

18. THE MOON

The unknown, illusion, psychic awareness, intuition, darkness, dark night of the soul, the void, subconscious, dreams, introspection, phases, divine feminine

Correspondences

- ✦ Celestial body/sign: Pisces
- ✦ Element: water
- ✦ Crystal: selenite
- ✦ Herb: lemon balm
- ✦ Oil: sandalwood

Imagery: A shining moon sits deep in concentration over a mountain path. Two pillars representing polarity, duality and a gateway, sit on either side of the path along with a tame dog and a wild wolf. From the water a crayfish emerges as a symbol for the emotional state or subconscious mind. The yods appear again, reminding you that you can find your way in times of darkness through your connection with divine guidance and trust in your intuition.

Empowering meanings

- ✦ The Moon doesn't give clear answers or direction but instead asks you to pause and look within. Learn to trust your intuition when the path ahead isn't clear.
- ✦ The answers you seek can only be found within you.
- ✦ You may need to just sit tight for now, having patience and waiting for the sun to rise on the issues at hand so you can clearly see your next step.

- All will be revealed in time.
- Be aware of how illusion may be affecting or impacting your choices in life.
- If you are going through a difficult time, remember that it's always darkest before the dawn.

Reversed meanings: Illusion controlling your decisions, not aware of or listening to your subconscious desires or guidance, not trusting your intuition. End of a long night or difficult time, the sun rising.

Inquiry questions
- What is unknown right now?
- How can I move forward when I can't see the path ahead?

Affirmations
- I am guided by my inner light.
- I trust my intuition.

Ritual: Sit in the darkness and listen to your inner wisdom. Light a candle to symbolise the dawn and divine light.

19. THE SUN

Optimism, joy, happiness, vitality, inner child, play, success, blessings, future success assured, magnetism, life, light, energy, ray of sunshine, glory, confidence, delight, brilliance, recognition, warmth, popularity, contentment, illumination, solar plexus chakra

Correspondences
- Celestial body/sign: sun
- Element: fire
- Crystal: sunstone
- Herb: bay laurel
- Oil: lemon verbena

Imagery: A bright sun shines down over a smiling child on a horse. The child's arms are outstretched, opening to blessings and happiness. A red banner waves on their side, a symbol of manifested success. Sunflowers grow along a wall behind, symbols of adoration, loyalty, happiness and joy. The half wall indicates that obstacles have been overcome.

Empowering meanings
- Happiness, joy and optimism are yours!
- Celebrate your successes, seek out and create things that bring you joy, give yourself permission to be happy and open yourself to receive blessings in all forms.
- Your inner child may be asking to come out to play, so do things that make life fun again.

- Live your life to the fullest. Say 'Yes' to things that excite and inspire you. Do things that make you feel happy and alive.
- Be grateful for all the light and love in your life and be open to experiencing even more of it.

Reversed meanings: Not seeing or accepting blessings, unhappiness and lack of joy, a need for inner child healing, feeling that you're never doing enough, lack of energy or inspiration. Overconfidence or too much ego.

Inquiry questions
- What makes me happy?
- How can I be more optimistic about life?

Affirmations
- I am the light.
- I am happy, joyful and successful!

Ritual: Visualise a bright sun shining bright on your solar plexus chakra.

20. JUDGEMENT

Spiritual awakening, redemption, karma, revelation, resurrection, renewal, realisation, spiritual calling, higher purpose, evaluation, phoenix rising from the ashes, judging others, being judged, a new era, rebirth, new phases

Correspondences
- Celestial body/sign: Pluto
- Element: fire
- Crystal: apophyllite
- Herb: hawthorn
- Oil: rosemary

Imagery: The symbolism of the Judgement card can seem a little bizarre at first: a group of dead, naked people standing up in their coffins as Archangel Gabriel blows a trumpet in the sky, depicting a biblical judgement day. The figures are experiencing a great revelation, representing freedom from the ties that bind, hope for the future and resurrection.

Empowering meanings
- This is a time of great spiritual awakening or deeper spiritual realisation. These experiences are not always easy to navigate, and you may have a feeling of loss or grief for the old ways of being as you move into higher consciousness and deeper spiritual awareness.
- This is a time of starting over, of second chances and redemption. If you have made some bad decisions and are

holding on to any guilt or shame, you're being asked to let that go now so you can be free to live with more ease and freedom.

✦ Watch how you judge yourself or others. Reflect on how you are living your life and, if you can, try to do better. If you need to make amends, do so.

✦ Don't hold on to resentment, pain or blame towards others or yourself. Make things right where you can or learn to let them go.

✦ It is time to let go of old ways of being and become new.

Reversed meanings: Resistance to moving on, blocking off from higher spiritual awareness, ignoring spiritual truths, judging yourself or others unfairly, holding guilt, blame or unforgiveness towards yourself or others.

Inquiry questions

✦ What guilt, blame or shame am I ready to let go of?

✦ How do I judge myself or others unfairly?

Affirmations

✦ I am awake and aware.

✦ I am liberated from old ways of being that no longer serve me.

Ritual: Write down the ways in which you judge yourself. Burn the paper and forgive yourself.

21. THE WORLD

Worldly success, achievement, triumph, potential reached, realisation of dreams, manifestation, dreams come true, celebration, rewards, travel, fulfilment, opportunity, destiny, you have arrived, the world is your oyster, infinite potential and possibility

Correspondences
- Celestial body/sign: Saturn
- Element: earth
- Crystal: hematite
- Herb: bay laurel
- Oil: cypress

Imagery: A woman partially dressed in a purple wreath, a symbol of wisdom and spirituality, dances with batons in each hand in the centre of a wreath, symbolic of victory, accomplishment, growth and evolution. Around her are the four cherubim, representing the four elements and signifying harmony, stability and manifestation of success in the material world.

Empowering meanings
- Celebrate your accomplishments, notice all the good in your life and all the desires that have manifested, wisdom you've gained and growth and success you've experienced.
- Remember what you once wanted and what you now have.
- Whatever you focus on now and next has huge potential for success.

- Be an active participant in your life and in your communities and the world around you. Put yourself out there and share your skills, talents and light with others.
- The world is your oyster! Enjoy your success, know your worth and get out there and make a positive difference in the world.

Reversed meanings: Not seeing or acknowledging your accomplishments or success, achievement of dreams or goals being delayed or blocked, withdrawing from the world, too much focus on the spiritual and not enough on the material plane, lack of belief in your self.

Inquiry questions
- How can I celebrate my successes and achievements?
- How can I reach my full potential?

Affirmations
- The world is my oyster.
- All my wildest dreams can come true.

Ritual: Carry a laurel or bay leaf with you as a talisman for worldly success.

Expanded card meanings

ACE OF WANDS

New beginnings and growth, sowing seeds, spark of inspiration, fertility, life force, creativity, power, will, excitement, passion

Correspondences
- Celestial body: Mars
- Signs: Aries, Leo, Sagittarius
- Element: fire
- Crystal: ruby
- Herb: pepper
- Oil: basil

Imagery: A disembodied hand appears from a cloud in the sky, presenting a wand with sprouting buds. This wand is a symbol of new beginnings, passion, power and will.

Empowering meanings
- Whether you are starting something new or starting over this is a time to pick up your wand, take the power into your own hands, follow your passions and take action!
- Believe in your ability to see this new opportunity, adventure or project through to completion.
- It's hard to ignore the phallic nature of this card and it may represent new sexual energy or different lovers.

Reversed meanings: Resistance to starting again, inability or unwillingness to take action and put the work in to see your dreams manifest.

Inquiry questions
+ What needs new growth in my life?
+ Where am I being called to take up my magic wand?

Affirmations
+ I can always begin again.
+ I am open to opportunities and take affirmative action.

Ritual: Write down your dreams, plant them with a seed then water and look after them.

TWO OF WANDS

Big dreams, planning, visualisation, manifestation, preparation for success, personal power, contemplation

Correspondences
- Celestial body: Mars
- Sign: Aries
- Element: fire
- Crystal: citrine
- Herb: bergamot
- Oil: peppermint

Imagery: A figure stands between two wands, a globe in one hand as a symbol of the world being in their hands. They look out at a vast horizon, representing their potential for success.

Empowering meanings
- Get clear about what it is you really want and then make a plan for how to make it happen. This is your planning, dreaming and visioning phase.
- Prepare for success and for all your dreams to come true.

Reversed meanings: An inability or resistance to making a plan, dropping the ball on plans, not taking time to prepare for the journey ahead.

Inquiry questions

✦ What am I visualising for the future?

✦ What is my plan for getting there?

Affirmations

✦ I am manifesting my dreams.

✦ I am preparing for my success.

Ritual: Write down where you are and where you want to be. Draw a line connecting them and visualise your path to success.

THREE OF WANDS

Holding the vision, ships coming in, hard work paying off, achievement, overseas travel, foresight, vision, enterprise, business and trade

Correspondences

- Celestial body: sun
- Sign: Aries
- Element: fire
- Crystal: aventurine
- Herb: saffron
- Oil: wild orange

Imagery: A figure is surrounded by three upright wands. He holds confidently on to one wand as he looks out over the sea where three ships that represent his goals and dreams are coming in.

Empowering meanings

- Acknowledge how far you've already come. Celebrate your wins and successes and the goals you have reached, but don't lose sight of the bigger picture. Keep holding your vision for success steady, and believe in yourself and your ability to manifest your biggest dreams.

Reversed meanings: Losing sight of your goals, resistance to success and achievement, focusing on someone else's dreams rather than your own.

Inquiry questions

✦ What visions am I holding?

✦ What goals or dreams have I lost sight of?

Affirmations

✦ My ships are coming in.

✦ I am so proud of all I've achieved so far.

Ritual: Create a message in a bottle or jar spell. Write down your desire on a piece of paper and put it in a bottle or jar along with any herbs, crystals, flowers or anything else you feel called to add. Keep it on your altar until your desire manifests.

FOUR OF WANDS

Home, security, stability, ceremony, celebration, abundance, home and property, wedding, events, completion, goals reached, harmony, happiness, firm foundations

Correspondences
- Celestial body: Venus
- Sign: Aries
- Element: fire
- Crystal: amber
- Herb: cumin
- Oil: marjoram

Imagery: Two figures hold up bouquets under an archway of four very stable-looking wands covered in garlands of flowers. A large gathering celebrates in front of the castle behind them, suggesting abundance, security and happiness.

Empowering meanings
- Count your blessings. Be grateful for the stability and abundance already in your life.
- Enjoy the fruits of your labour and celebrate good times with friends and family.
- This is a very positive card to see if you are asking about your home, property or marriage.

Reversed meanings: Events not going to plan, feeling unstable, challenges with your home or a property, lack of celebration of the good things in life.

Inquiry questions
+ What is stable in my life?
+ How can I feel stable, safe and secure in times of uncertainty?

Affirmations
+ I am safe and secure.
+ I celebrate good times.

Ritual: Create a playlist of happy celebration songs and dance to them often!

FIVE OF WANDS

Conflict, competition, power struggles, differing opinions, frustration, inability to see the viewpoints of others, annoyances, quarrels, confrontation, inner conflict

Correspondences

- Celestial body: Saturn
- Sign: Leo
- Element: fire
- Crystal: labradorite
- Herb: nettle
- Oil: patchouli

Imagery: Five figures hold up wands at different angles and appear to be struggling to work together to achieve a common or individual goal or purpose.

Empowering meanings

- Look at where you're in conflict within yourself, which will often be where your biggest challenges and opportunities for growth and change are.
- When dealing with conflict with others you may need to step up and be the bigger person.
- Get organised and stop wasting time on anything that's going nowhere.
- Make sure you're not pushing your agenda on others or letting others force theirs on you.

Reversed meanings: An end to conflict, compromise, things falling back into place after a challenging time, loosening your grip to control a situation or others.

Inquiry questions
✦ Where am I in conflict with others?

✦ Where am I in conflict within myself?

Affirmations
✦ All my relationships are harmonious.

✦ I listen to others, and I am heard by others.

Ritual: Organise your sock, cutlery or desk drawer.

SIX OF WANDS

Victory, recognition, validation, success, confidence, self-esteem, leadership, popularity, fame, honour, pride, triumph

Correspondences

- Celestial body: Jupiter
- Sign: Leo
- Element: fire
- Crystal: imperial or golden topaz
- Herb: laurel
- Oil: tangerine

Imagery: A figure wearing a laurel wreath, a symbol of victory, sits confidently on a horse and is holding a wand with another laurel wreath on top as they ride back into town after winning a battle. Five wands are held up by a group that is celebrating this person's success.

Empowering meanings

- Accept, honour and recognise your successes. Be proud of yourself for all you've achieved.
- More victory and recognition can be yours if you believe in yourself and your ability to succeed.
- Validation may come from others, but validate yourself first!

Reversed meanings: Not seeing or accepting the recognition being handed to you, resistance to accepting compliments and a lack of self-esteem, seeing something as a failure rather than a learning opportunity.

Inquiry questions

✦ Where am I not recognising my achievements?

✦ How can I own my success?

Affirmations

✦ I am victorious!

✦ I acknowledge and celebrate my achievements.

Ritual: Visualise the word 'victory' written in gold on your forehead.

Expanded card meanings

SEVEN OF WANDS

Perseverance, persistence, holding ground, taking a stand, defending yourself and others, fighting for what you believe in, overcoming the odds, determination, facing challenges head on, integrity

Correspondences
- Celestial body: Mars
- Sign: Leo
- Element: fire
- Crystal: tourmaline
- Herb: bay leaf
- Oil: cypress

Imagery: A figure stands on a hilltop brandishing a wand in a powerful stance of focus and determination. Six wands appear from below trying to push the person off their position, but the figure holds their ground and stays strong.

Empowering meanings
- Now is not the time to quit: it's time to reach into your inner reserves and keep going.
- Fight for what you want and don't let others get to you. Your persistence will pay off if you just keep holding your ground and fighting for what matters most to you.
- There may be people around you who want to see you fail. Don't give them the satisfaction!

Reversed meanings: Giving up on something that was important to you, losing faith in your dreams or yourself, others bringing you down.

Inquiry questions
✦ Who or what am I fighting for or against?

✦ How can I keep going when I want to give up?

Affirmations
✦ I show up for and protect what's important to me.

✦ I stand up for what I believe in.

Ritual: Support a cause you believe in through donations or signing and sharing petitions.

Expanded card meanings

195

EIGHT OF WANDS

Alignment, swift action, fast movement, speed, clear path ahead, potential, direction, focused intention and energy, progress, inspiration

Correspondences
- Celestial body: Mercury
- Sign: Sagittarius
- Element: fire
- Crystal: fluorite
- Herb: ginger
- Oil: pine

Imagery: Eight wands fly swiftly through the sky in a perfectly aligned formation. This is a card of speed, movement and alignment.

Empowering meanings
- Focus on aligning your energy, thoughts, intentions and actions so things move more effortlessly and easily.
- Get into alignment with your dreams and desires and then give them that push they need in order for them to manifest.

Reversed meanings: Blocked, stuck, slow or stagnant energy, not enough push to get the wands off the ground, aiming in the wrong direction.

TAROT CARD COMPANION

Inquiry questions

✦ Where am I aiming my focus and energy?

✦ How can I align myself to what I want?

Affirmations

✦ My energy is focused and aligned.

✦ Things move quickly and easily for me.

Ritual: Align your chakras.

NINE OF WANDS

Resilience, staying the course, weariness, seeing things through, responsibility, discipline, dedication, persistence, strength, fighting the good fight, determination

Correspondences

- Celestial body: moon
- Sign: Sagittarius
- Element: fire
- Crystal: astrophyllite
- Herb: mustard seed
- Oil: cypress

Imagery: A figure stands holding on to or leaning on a wand while another eight wands stand behind them. Their head is bandaged and they appear to be a little worse for wear and battle weary, but they are still holding strong! They seem exhausted and injured, but there is no indication at all that they are about to give up. They are going to see this thing through to its final conclusion.

Empowering meanings

- If you've been feeling weary or as though you've been working very hard for a long time to manifest or create something that is yet to come to fruition, keep holding strong.
- Discipline and responsibility are needed now. There may be things that need your attention that you'd really rather walk

away from, but it's important that you show up, stay true to your word and do what you need to do.

+ Something may need finishing: work or creative projects, study, online courses or books you haven't finished.

+ There is magic in seeing things through and getting things done.

Reversed meanings: Giving up or letting go too soon, an inability or choice not to see a project or situation to its final conclusion or manifestation.

Inquiry questions
+ How can I stand strong in this situation?
+ What support do I need to make it through this final push?

Affirmations
+ I am rewarded when I stay the course.
+ I see things through.

Ritual: Do something you've said you would do but haven't yet got around to.

TEN OF WANDS

Burdens, obligation, duty, final push, taking on too much, doing everything yourself, weight on your shoulders, responsibilities, commitment to seeing things through

Correspondences
- Celestial body: Saturn
- Sign: Sagittarius
- Element: fire
- Crystal: labradorite
- Herb: dandelion
- Oil: rosemary

Imagery: A bent-over figure carries a heavy load of 10 wands towards a town in the distance. The wands obstruct their view, suggesting they may not be able to clearly see to the end of this situation.

Empowering meanings
- You may be taking too much responsibility onto your shoulders. If you can, put down this heavy load.
- If you have a duty to or no choice to walk away from what you carry, know that you are nearing the end of this cycle. This is not a forever kind of situation: at some point soon you will be able to put this burden down.
- Let go of any old emotional baggage from the past that is preventing you moving forward.

- A final push may be needed to help you reach your destination.
- If you need to let go, let go. If you need to push through, keep going because you're nearly there!

Reversed meanings: Something released and let go, a relief or removal of stress and burden, giving up just before the end.

Inquiry questions
- What is weighing me down?
- What can I let go of?

Affirmations
- There is light at the end of this tunnel.
- I let go of what weighs me down.

Ritual: Remove something from your to-do list.

PAGE OF WANDS

Adventurous, curious, excited about life, passionate, ambitious, hot tempered, movement, new beginnings, travel, creativity, future focused, study

Correspondences

- Celestial body: sun
- Signs: Aries, Leo, Sagittarius
- Elements: earth, fire
- Crystal: yellow calcite
- Herb: borage
- Oil: lime

Imagery: The Page of Wands stands tall, confident and determined with a wand steady in their hands. The orange sand beneath their feet and the pyramids in the background tells us this Page is already on an adventure, travelling to distant lands and learning all they can about the world.

As a person: This is a young person who is passionate, driven, excited by life and loves travel, especially backpacking and going off the beaten path. They often have no interest in staying in one place or sitting still for too long, as there is just too much to experience and learn!

Their shadow traits can include difficulties sticking to their studies or committing to relationships. They are always looking for the next new shiny thing.

Empowering meanings
- It's time for adventure and to get excited about life again. Plan that trip you've been thinking about or follow new, exciting paths that are calling to you.
- Remember that the magic is always found outside your comfort zone.

Reversed meanings: Resisting change or new beginnings, disconnection from your true passions and purpose, feeling lost or not at home in this world, not listening to the nudges and guidance calling you forward.

Inquiry questions
- What am I excited about?
- What adventures are calling me?

Affirmations
- I follow my passions.
- I am ready for a new adventure.

Ritual: Create a vision board for your travels and adventures.

Expanded card meanings

KNIGHT OF WANDS

Courageous, confident, enthusiastic, brave, vibrant, fiery, changeable, charismatic, revolutionary, proud, competitive, dynamic, charming, adding spice to your life

Correspondences
- Celestial body: Mars
- Sign: Sagittarius
- Elements: air, fire
- Crystal: Libyan desert glass
- Herb: cayenne pepper
- Oil: petitgrain

Imagery: The Knight of Wands wears armour with fiery plumes as he brandishes a wand in the air. His horse rears, suggesting fiery forward movement. In the distance pyramids can again be seen, a symbol of adventure and travel.

As a person: This is someone who has passion, conviction and great courage to pursue their dreams. They will not hesitate to take action for themselves or on behalf of others. Adventurous and enthusiastic, they can be an absolute joy to be around but you may find they aren't around for long!

Their shadow traits include difficulties committing, getting bored easily, not sticking to a task or goal or struggling to stay in one place, job or relationship for a long period of time.

Empowering meanings

✦ Be brave and courageous in your life. Follow your passions and let the things that light you up lead the way.

✦ Look for ways to be of service to others, your community and the world. Being of service will fulfil you in wonderful ways.

Reversed meanings: Letting fear stop you from living your dreams, ignoring your passions, lack of confidence in yourself or your abilities, a potential to be too fiery, burn out or not stick something out.

Inquiry questions

✦ Where do I need more courage?

✦ How am I being called to be of service?

Affirmations

✦ I am brave and courageous.

✦ I am of service.

Ritual: Light a candle, and affirm as the candle burns down that your courage and confidence will increase.

QUEEN OF WANDS

Passionate, inspirational, warm, courageous, creative, magnetic, kind, commanding, adaptable, energetic, confident, strong-willed, extroverted, optimistic

Correspondences

- Celestial body: Venus
- Sign: Aries
- Elements: water, fire
- Crystal: fire agate
- Herb: sweet basil
- Oil: angelica root

Imagery: The Queen of Wands sits on a throne with her wand in one hand and a sunflower, symbolising vitality, optimism, joy and strength, in the other. Lions appear on her throne and behind her, representing strength and courage. A small black cat sits at her feet, symbolising the occult and esoteric energy.

As a person: This is someone who is hopeful and optimistic, follows her own passions and supports others in following theirs. Queen of Wands people are warm, big hearted, kind and compassionate. They always make you feel at home, loved and cared for, and if they push you out of your comfort zone at times it's only because they want you to succeed.

In their shadow aspect they may be pushy, emotionally explosive, have no patience with themselves or others and struggle to express their needs and wants in positive ways.

Empowering meanings

✦ This is a positive and hopeful time. You have achieved so much, stood strong and showed courage and now you're being asked to show up in even bigger ways: leading, supporting and inspiring others to do what you have done.

✦ You have the confidence and courage to do anything you set your mind to now. Keep following your dreams, forging out paths towards new ones and inspiring all those around you in the process.

✦ You are a radiant light and people love being in your presence.

Reversed meanings: Avoiding leadership responsibilities or opportunities, letting others down, letting yourself down, not seeing how strong, courageous and capable you are.

Inquiry questions

✦ How have your strength and confidence grown?

✦ How are you being called to inspire others?

Affirmations

✦ I am inspirational.

✦ I radiate warmth, light and joy.

Ritual: Share some inspirational guidance on social media or with a friend who needs it.

KING OF WANDS

Loyal, dynamic, assertive, visionary, impactful leader, fearless, strong, honest, impulsive, protective, charismatic, adventurous, dominant, forceful, self-directed, responsible, virile

Correspondences

- Celestial body: Jupiter
- Sign: Leo
- Element: fire
- Crystal: heliodor
- Herb: vervain
- Oil: cedarwood

Imagery: The King of Wands sits on his throne with a wand in one hand. He appears confident and assured in his place as a leader, and ready to jump in and take action at any moment. Lions adorn the back of his throne, symbolising courage, and a salamander, the symbol of fire, sits at his feet.

As a person: A King of Wands person is loyal, strong, brave and fiery. They may be a member of the military, a leader in their profession or someone with much expertise and experience to share with others. Ready to step up and fight for what they believe in, they will always have your back and will support and defend you in a heartbeat.

Their shadow aspects can include being too aggressive or hot headed or they may rush into dangerous situations.

Empowering meanings

✦ You have faced your fears, been tried and tested and come out winning. You have gained strength of will and heart and can now lead the way for others. Your spiritual maturity is an inspiration for many.

✦ You have followed your passions, taken action and manifested wonderful things in your life. Now it's time to help and support others to do the same.

✦ Keep living your life with courage!

Reversed meanings: Not seeing how far you've come on your journey, not realising how much you influence and impact others, a negative influence or effect on others, losing your spark, impatience, hot headedness.

Inquiry questions

✦ What am I willing to protect and work hard for?

✦ How can I achieve greater spiritual maturity?

Affirmations

✦ I inspire others to live a passionate life.

✦ I am assertive.

Ritual: Support someone who is trying to live their dreams through advice, guidance or words of encouragement.

ACE OF CUPS

Self-love, self-care, heart opening, well-being, fulfilment, endless supply from source energy, blessings, holy grail, spiritual nourishment, opening of psychic channels, emotions

Correspondences
- Celestial body: Venus
- Signs: Cancer, Libra, Scorpio
- Element: water
- Crystal: rhodochrosite
- Herb: hawthorn
- Oil: palmarosa

Imagery: A hand emerges from a cloud holding a cup that is full and overflowing with water, suggesting fulfilment, blessings and endless supply. The dove, a symbol of the Holy Spirit, above the cup represents spiritual nourishment.

Empowering meanings:
- There is potential here for you to receive many blessings, especially when it comes to love, wellness and fulfilment.
- Fill your own cup first. When you look after yourself, love yourself and focus on your well-being you become just like the Ace of Cups: a vessel overflowing with love and blessings that ripple out and serves all those you meet on the path.

+ When you love and care for yourself your heart opens and you become a magnet for love and blessings in all forms.

Reversed meanings: An empty cup, nothing more to give, putting others first to your own detriment. Being overly emotional or a cup overflowing with negative emotions.

Inquiry questions
+ What fulfils you?
+ What provides you with spiritual nourishment?

Affirmations
+ My cup runneth over.
+ I am overflowing with love and blessings!

Ritual: Hold a glass of water in both hands and visualise it full of well-being, love, prosperity and opportunities. Drink it.

TWO OF CUPS

Positive partnerships, kindred spirits, connection, collaboration, romance, balanced feminine and masculine, emotional balance, dating, fulfilling relationships, balanced energy exchange, sexual attraction, mutual respect

Correspondences
- Celestial body: Venus
- Sign: Libra
- Element: water
- Crystal: rhodochrosite
- Herb: vanilla
- Oil: neroli

Imagery: Two figures stand facing each other, each holding a cup in their hands. One reaches gently forward. The lion's head above represents passion and strength in relationships while the wings and caduceus are symbols of Hermes or Mercury, the god of communication.

Empowering meanings
- Be open to new love, friendships, relationships or collaborations. Reach out to those you'd like to have a stronger connection with and be open to others when they reach out to you.
- Support others and let others support you. You do not have to do things on your own: let people help and support you.
- Be open to kindred spirits coming into your life.

✦ This is a very positive card for new love and first dates!

Reversed meanings: A challenging or unbalanced relationship with not enough give and take, a need to put more effort into your relationships or a resistance to reaching out or creating deeper connections with others.

Inquiry questions
✦ Who are you being called to reach out to?
✦ How or where may you find kindred spirits?

Affirmations
✦ My relationships are fulfilling.
✦ I attract kindred spirits into my life.

Ritual: Send a text or voice note to someone you would like a deeper connection with.

THREE OF CUPS

Friendship, abundance, celebration, joy, support, gratitude, pleasure, happy times, a good harvest, bonding with others, rituals, gatherings or events

Correspondences
- Celestial body: Mercury
- Sign: Cancer
- Element: water
- Crystal: shattuckite
- Herb: cardamom
- Oil: rose geranium

Imagery: Three figures hold up their cups in a joyful toast, and around their feet are many fruits of abundance. These good friends are celebrating all they have, all they've created, and are supporting each other's success.

Empowering meanings
- Spend time with people who fill and light you up, support you and celebrate your successes.
- Celebrate others and support those around you. Remember that a rising tide lifts all boats, so congratulate those who are doing well and more abundance will surely come your way.

✦ Seek joy, count your blessings, be grateful for what you have. Spend more time doing the things that make you happy. This is one of the fastest ways to feel more abundant.

Reversed meanings: Not recognising or celebrating your success or the successes of others, comparison or competition with others, struggling to notice your abundance.

Inquiry questions
✦ How can you support the successes of your friends and loved ones?
✦ What rituals can help you celebrate yourself and others going forward?

Affirmations
✦ I am abundant.
✦ I choose to spend my time with people who lift me up.

Ritual: Reach out to a friend and plan a get-together.

FOUR OF CUPS

Dissatisfaction, boredom, withdrawal, discontent, inability to see what's right in front of you, apathy, daydreams, pity party, possibilities and potentials, self-absorption, being over it

Correspondences
- Celestial body: moon
- Sign: Cancer
- Element: water
- Crystal: faden quartz
- Herb: St John's wort
- Oil: helichrysum

Imagery: A figure sits under a tree with their arms crossed and head down. Three cups sit at a distance in front, while another cup goes completely unnoticed appearing out of a cloud in the sky.

Empowering meanings
- This is your wake-up call. If things haven't been as successful or wonderful as you'd hoped for, take time to feel your feelings but don't stay too long in your pity party. You're unable to see all the good that's still right in front of you or the wonderful new things coming in.
- This is just a little blip on your path. Good things are coming, so stay open to receiving and to new possibilities, help, support and guidance.

TAROT CARD COMPANION

Reversed meanings: Coming out of a fog or a time when you've felt sorry for yourself, being able to see clearly again, being open to and taking up opportunities.

Inquiry questions

- ✦ What am I not seeing?
- ✦ Where am I closed off to receiving gifts and good things?

Affirmations

- ✦ I am open to receiving gifts and opportunities.
- ✦ I see things clearly and am open to new possibilities.

Ritual: Open your arms wide and affirm: 'I am open to blessings, gifts, opportunities and all good things.'

FIVE OF CUPS

Disappointment, regret, glass half empty, loss, crying over spilt milk, letting go, progress hindered, delay, learning from experience and mistakes, silver linings

Correspondences
- Celestial body: Mars
- Sign: Scorpio
- Element: water
- Crystal: ocean jasper
- Herb: skullcap
- Oil: blue tansy

Imagery: A figure stands by a river in a long, dark cloak. Their head is bowed in sadness as they look at three cups that have spilled over and poured out. Behind them are two upright cups still standing. In the distance can be seen a house and bridge, symbolising perhaps a need to cross a bridge or get over something.

Empowering meanings
- Let yourself grieve for what you've lost. You are allowed to feel sad and upset about things that haven't worked out, dreams that failed or people who are no longer in your life, but don't lose sight of the bigger picture. There is still goodness, people to love, dreams to work towards and so much to be grateful for if you take the time to look for it.
- Let the past go, turn around and focus on the future.

Reversed meanings: A very difficult loss, ability to move on, emotional healing, being ready to turn things around, focusing on what you have rather than what is lost.

Inquiry questions
✦ What have I lost?
✦ What good still remains?

Affirmations
✦ There is so much good in my life.
✦ I am grateful for what I have.

Ritual: Write a gratitude list.

SIX OF CUPS

Generosity, gifts, inner child, nostalgia, harmony, innocence, childhood, happy memories, old friends, giving, reminiscing

Correspondences

- Celestial body: sun
- Sign: Scorpio
- Element: water
- Crystal: tangerine quartz
- Herb: marshmallow root
- Oil: mandarin

Imagery: A child stands in a marketplace with their nose in a full cup of white flowers, which are symbolic of innocence and purity. Another cup of flowers stands behind them and four more sit on the ground. It appears as though they may be gifting these flowers to an older woman in the square, symbolising the passage of time.

Empowering meanings

- Be generous with your love, time and energy. Send gifts or messages of love and support to old friends.
- Connect with your inner child. Bring play, fun and happiness back into your life.

✦ Enjoy memories of the good old days and bring those good feelings into the present so you can create more good times here and now.

Reversed meanings: Difficulties with giving or receiving, neglecting your inner child, too much work and not enough play, living in the past.

Inquiry questions
✦ What does my inner child need from me right now?
✦ What can I do now to support my future self?

Affirmations
✦ I am generous with my time, love and energy.
✦ I honour, love and listen to my inner child.

Ritual: Watch a television show or movie you loved as a child or teen.

SEVEN OF CUPS

Choosing wisely, reality vs illusion, possibilities, desires, imagination, fantasy, choice overwhelm, pipe dreams, wishful thinking, temptation, indulgence

Correspondences
- Celestial body: Venus
- Sign: Pisces
- Element: water
- Crystal: azurite
- Herb: blue vervain
- Oil: Roman chamomile

Imagery: A darkened figure is presented with seven cups, each containing a different choice, opportunity or path. The cups contain a woman's face (representing love or beauty), a snake (temptation or knowledge), a castle (a big home), a pile of jewels (riches), a wreath (success and victory) and a dragon (power, danger or transformation), and in the very centre is a mysterious shrouded figure (the unknown).

Empowering meanings
- A choice needs to be made. Pause and consider what you really want and what is the true cost of it. Are you choosing what your heart and soul most want or are you choosing what you think or have been told will make you happy?

◆ Consider things carefully and avoid making a hasty choice. Choose from your heart, not your ego.

Reversed meanings: Resistance to making a choice resulting in possible stagnation, feeling overwhelmed by choices, worry or anxiety over which choice to make.

Inquiry questions
◆ What does my ego want?
◆ What do my heart and soul want?

Affirmations
◆ I trust myself to choose the right path.
◆ I trust I will always be guided to make the right decisions.

Ritual: Pull a tarot card on each option that is available to you.

EIGHT OF CUPS

Letting go, leaving the past behind, spiritual journey or quest, a search for meaning, following a calling, finding yourself, soul searching, healing journey, decluttering, minimalism

Correspondences
+ Celestial body: Saturn
+ Sign: Pisces
+ Element: water
+ Crystal: azurite
+ Herb: elderflower
+ Oil: blue chamomile

Imagery: Eight cups are stacked neatly in the foreground as though the cloaked figure has left behind what they no longer need or want and then begun to walk towards the mountains, a symbol of a journey or spiritual path.

Empowering meanings
+ Leave behind you what no longer serves or supports you and go in search of something more meaningful.
+ You may feel called to take a journey of self-discovery to find yourself or a deeper part of yourself, or perhaps even to go on a spiritual quest of some kind.
+ There may be a need to release and heal from the past in order to walk a higher and happier path.

✦ There are times in life when you must journey alone; this may be one of them.

Reversed meanings: Resistance to taking a journey that your soul is craving, putting others ahead of your healing journey, not taking time for your spiritual practice, resistance to walking the spiritual path.

Inquiry questions
✦ What are you searching for?
✦ What do you need to leave behind so you can move forward?

Affirmations
✦ I walk my own path.
✦ I let go and move on.

Ritual: Take a walk in nature with no headphones or other distractions: just you and your journey.

NINE OF CUPS

Contentment, gratitude, wishes fulfilled, achievement, success, enjoying life's pleasures, financial stability, satisfaction, fruition, material happiness, material gain, enjoyment of life

Correspondences
- Celestial body: Jupiter
- Sign: Pisces
- Element: water
- Crystal: green calcite
- Herb: borage
- Oil: copaiba

Imagery: A well-dressed figure sits on a bench with their arms crossed, looking very happy, relaxed and proud. Nine cups sit on a shelf above them like trophies. They appear to be very pleased and content with all they have achieved and all the material gains they have made.

Empowering meanings
- Your wish has been granted, so count your blessings. Appreciate all you have, celebrate how far you've come and trust and know that there is always more available to you.
- If you wish for something you don't yet have, stay present to the blessings all around you while you wait for it come into your life. Don't tell yourself you'll be happy when . . .; choose to be happy now.

✦ This is a very positive card to see in any reading.

Reversed meanings: An inability to see the blessings and abundance already in your life, a resistance to receiving or difficulty holding on to what you've received.

Inquiry questions
✦ What is your wish?
✦ How can you choose to be happy here and now?

Affirmations
✦ I am grateful for all the abundance in my life.
✦ My wishes always come true.

Ritual: Make a wish on a star, wish candle or dandelion.

TEN OF CUPS

Dreams come true, happily ever after, happy home life, loving family, fulfilment, good fortune, love, friendship, goals reached, happiness, blessings

Correspondences

- Celestial body: Mars
- Sign: Pisces
- Element: water
- Crystal: ametrine
- Herb: hibiscus
- Oil: elemi

Imagery: A happy couple stand under a rainbow of 10 full cups, their arms around each other and open in a gesture of receptivity and gratitude. Two children play happily by their side and a small house stands in the distance.

Empowering meanings

- Prayers are answered, dreams are coming true and desires are manifested. Happiness, happy home life and good fortune are yours.
- Remember that the greatest wealth in this world is love.
- Enjoy quality time with the people you love and care about: your friends, family, found family and animal companions.
- Your dreams are manifesting or are in reach. Enjoy this magical time.

Reversed meanings: An inability or resistance to see the good in your life, feeling as though you never have enough, discontentment in your family or home life or dreams not being realised: yet!

Inquiry questions
+ In what ways am I already blessed?
+ What blessings am I calling in?

Affirmations
+ I am loved, safe and happy.
+ All my dreams are coming true.

Ritual: Visualise a rainbow over your home.

PAGE OF CUPS

Unique, artistic, light-hearted, inspirational, creative, quirky, intuitive, self-expressive, sensitive, dreamy, imaginative, kind, considerate, helpful, psychic

Correspondences

- Celestial body: moon
- Signs: Cancer, Scorpio, Pisces
- Elements: earth, water
- Crystal: apatite
- Herb: hawthorn berry
- Oil: pink grapefruit

Imagery: A young man stands in front of a body of water holding a cup containing a speaking fish. His stance suggests a playful and easy attitude. He appears to be a quirky character, one who is not afraid to express his true self or listen to the wisdom of the animals.

As a person: This young person is creative and expressive, maybe a little quirky, is guided by their emotions and is generous, loving and heart-centred.

Their shadow aspects can include becoming moody and self-defeating, judging themselves too harshly, feeling their creative work is no good, comparing themselves with others and withdrawing into their own world.

Empowering meanings

✦ Embrace your uniqueness and shine your light in the way only you can. Follow your creative passions and express the truth of who you really are through creative projects and in the way you live your life.

✦ Share your unique perspective with others and don't be afraid to be yourself and show the world the real you.

✦ It is a fantastic time to learn a new creative skill or embrace a different artistic hobby.

Reversed meanings: Not being true to who you are, hiding or dimming your light to make others feel more comfortable, ignoring the divine sparks of inspiration, not making time for creative projects, letting others define who you are.

Inquiry questions

✦ In what ways do I dim my light to fit in or hide my light?

✦ How can I express the truth of who I am more fully?

Affirmations

✦ I am creative.

✦ I am unique and interesting and wonderful.

Ritual: Dress to express yourself.

KNIGHT OF CUPS

Heart-led, loving, romantic, kind, open hearted, compassionate, intuitive, dreamy, calm, emotionally available, sensitive, knight in shining armour

Correspondences

- Celestial body: Venus
- Sign: Pisces
- Elements: air, water
- Crystal: morganite
- Herb: linden flower
- Oil: spikenard

Imagery: A knight in shining armour sits confidently on his horse and is holding a cup in front of his heart, showing us that his heart, emotions and intuition are leading him. The horse has one foot in the air, suggesting a steady walking pace as they travel over a river, a symbol of emotions and intuition.

As a person: A Knight of Cups person is heart-centred, kind, compassionate, romantic and more interested in following their heart than trends, money, fame or illusionary success. They wear their heart on their sleeve and have no problem showing their emotions and sharing their feelings with others.

Their shadow aspects include becoming obsessive or overly attached, holding on to past hurts for too long or being overly emotional.

Empowering meanings

✦ Follow your heart. Listen to your inner guidance and wisdom and go where you are guided.

✦ Be open to new love coming in: romantic, friendships and deeper self-love.

✦ Trust that things are moving forward, even if not as quickly as you'd like. Take your time; there is no rush.

✦ This is a positive card to see in matters of the heart and can symbolise a knight in shining armour coming into your life or the realisation that you can be the hero and saviour in your own story!

Reversed meanings: Closing your heart, ignoring your heart's callings, resistance or inability to share your emotions with others, not wanting or being able to put yourself out there, potential difficulties in romance due to not being honest about your feelings.

Inquiry questions

✦ How can I have the courage to follow my heart?

✦ How can I open my heart to receiving more love?

Affirmations

✦ I follow my heart.

✦ I am open to receiving love in all forms.

Ritual: Take yourself on a date: romance yourself!

QUEEN OF CUPS

Intuitive, compassionate, sensitive, psychic, nurturing, loving, wise, above reproach, devoted, dreamy, empathetic, creative, receptive, enchanting, spiritual, healer

Correspondences

- Celestial body: moon
- Sign: Cancer
- Element: water
- Crystal: danburite
- Herb: rose otto
- Oil: myrrh

Imagery: A queen sits on a throne half in water and half in sand, telling us she is attuned to her psychic abilities but also grounded in reality. She holds a large ornate cup in her hands, a symbol of intuition, psychic awareness and emotions, and appears to be enthralled by its beauty and importance.

As a person: A Queen of Cups person is loving, generous and compassionate. They are deeply intuitive, psychic, empathetic, understanding and wise and nurturing. Queen of Cups people run very deep and often enjoy their alone time in meditation or pondering on the mysteries of the universe. They have healing gifts, and you may feel better just by being in their presence.

In their shadow they can people please, find it difficult to set boundaries or give so much of their energy away to others they can become depleted.

Empowering meanings

✦ Listen to your intuition and trust it; you are more intuitive than you realise. You don't need anyone else's advice or opinion, you just need to trust yourself and be the queen of your heart, emotions and life.

✦ Be loving and compassionate towards yourself and others.

✦ Hold space for others and listen and support their healing journey in whatever way you can.

✦ Love fiercely but set clear, strong, healthy boundaries with others so you don't deplete your energy.

Reversed meanings: Disconnected from or not trusting your intuition, ignoring intuitive insights or guidance, running out of energy or giving too much of yourself away.

Inquiry questions

✦ How can I trust my intuition?

✦ How can I set loving boundaries with others?

Affirmations

✦ I am intuitive.

✦ I trust my intuition and myself.

Ritual: Place one hand on your heart and one on your belly. Sit quietly, take a deep breath and listen to your inner wisdom.

Expanded card meanings

KING OF CUPS

Psychic, empathetic, wise, supportive, understanding, heart-centred leader, artistic, responsible, calm, loyal, sincere, respected, a good adviser, emotional maturity

Correspondences

- Celestial body: Jupiter
- Sign: Scorpio
- Elements: fire, water
- Crystal: rhodonite
- Herb: red clover
- Oil: rosewood

Imagery: The King of Cups sits with confidence on his ocean throne. One toe is dipped towards the water, symbolising that he relies on his intuition in all things, especially leadership. He holds a cup, signifying his connection with love, intuition and his emotions, and a sceptre, a symbol of his maturity and mastery.

As a person: A King of Cups person is psychic, intuitive and empathetic and a heart-centred leader. They are deeply in tune with their emotions and express their feelings in mature and positive ways. They are often interested in art, storytelling, music and other creative pursuits.

Their shadow aspects include struggling to deal with their emotions, becoming withdrawn, being prone to depression or finding ways to numb themselves so they don't have to feel quite so much.

Empowering meanings

✦ You will require emotional mastery in this situation. Connect with your heart, soul and emotions. Listen to them, honour them and work with, not against them. Be honest about how you are feeling and express those feelings in healthy ways.

✦ Be a positive leader and role model for others by always leading from love.

Reversed meanings: Difficulties in expressing your emotions, bottling things up, trying too hard to make everyone around you happy at the cost of your own happiness, resistance to doing healing work, looking for ways to numb out.

Inquiry questions

✦ How can I live from my heart?

✦ How can I support others in following their hearts?

Affirmations

✦ I honour my emotions.

✦ I choose love.

Ritual: Take a ritual bath and be open to the guidance that comes while you are in the water.

Expanded card meanings

237

ACE OF SWORDS

New ideas, mental power, clarity, breakthrough, truth, logic, rationality, new ways of thinking, energy clearing, breath of fresh air

Correspondences
- Celestial body: Mercury
- Signs: Gemini, Libra, Aquarius
- Element: air
- Crystal: clear quartz point
- Herb: holy basil
- Oil: coriander

Imagery: A hand appears out of a cloud holding a sword crowned with a wreath of victory. The sword is a symbol of the mental realm, communication and power.

Empowering meanings
- Take back, activate and stay in your power: there is great potential here for breakthroughs and success. Be open to new ideas and fresh opportunities.
- Shift your mindset into one of success and victory. Speak your truth openly and honestly.
- Believe that you have the power, that you can win and you will! Your mindset is everything.

Reversed meanings: Harmful or negative thoughts about yourself or others, a negative mindset, giving your power away, not speaking up or sharing your truth, inability to believe in yourself.

Inquiry questions
✦ Is my mind a fertile ground for success and victory?
✦ How can I take back my power from my thoughts?

Affirmations
✦ I have the power!
✦ I speak my truth with love.

Ritual: Visualise white light clearing through your physical body, mind, crown chakra and aura.

Expanded card meanings

TWO OF SWORDS

Indecision, uncertainty, doubt, stalemate, duality, crossroads, trust, divine timing, consideration, finding answers within, compromise, protection

Correspondences
- Celestial body: moon
- Sign: Libra
- Element: air
- Crystal: staurolite
- Herb: rosemary
- Oil: myrtle

Imagery: A figure sits on a beach – the water is symbolic of the subconscious – under a crescent moon, a symbol of a new phase. With a sword in each hand, arms crossed at the heart centre and a blindfold over their face, they appear stuck in this place of indecision.

Empowering meanings
- Take your time figuring things out. Action is not yet required. This is a time for consideration, not a time to rush in. Meditate on the issue at hand so you can make decisions from a calm, clear place.
- You may need to seek out some extra information or impartial, practical guidance.

- Use both logic and intuition to guide you forward.
- You will figure things out. Take your time. Trust in divine timing and in your ability to make the right choice.

Reversed meanings: Making a quick decision, seeing things clearly, moving forward, possibly regretting a decision, changing your mind, going back on your choices.

Inquiry questions
- Where am I stuck in indecision, and how could I shift this energy?
- What extra information or support do I need to make this decision?

Affirmations
- I have permission to take my time making important decisions.
- I cannot make a wrong decision.

Ritual: Write a list of pros and cons for any decisions you are trying to make.

THREE OF SWORDS

Heartache, healing journey, heart-healing, separation, forgiveness, a need for self-care, self-love, self-compassion, sadness, sorrow

Correspondences
- Celestial body: Saturn
- Sign: Libra
- Element: air
- Crystal: Apache tears
- Herb: licorice root
- Oil: clary sage

Imagery: Three swords pierce a heart while dark clouds gather in the background as it rains down. While the storm clouds seem ominous, rain is a symbol of intuition and emotions and is also a healing force washing away any sadness or sorrow.

Empowering meanings
- Focus on your healing journey, self-love, self-care and helping yourself through any difficult time you are facing.
- Traditionally, this card is said to represent heartbreak and sorrow, but it is found in the suit of air (mind), not water (emotions), inviting you to consider that sometimes it's your own thoughts and mindset that cause you the most grief.
- Whatever is hurting can be healed. Take time out to focus on your emotional and mental well-being.

Reversed meanings: You have healed or are healing, a release or relief of suffering or sorrow, finding happiness again, mending your heart, dealing with or working through a break-up, healing from loss and moving on.

Inquiry questions
+ What thoughts are causing me suffering?
+ How can I gift myself more self-care and support?

Affirmations
+ I am on my healing journey.
+ I am healed and whole.

Ritual: Blend clary sage and rose oil with a carrier oil. Rub onto your heart twice daily.

FOUR OF SWORDS

Rest, recovery, relaxation, rejuvenation, retreat, pause, honouring yourself, taking time out, refuge, solace, peace, meditation, tranquility, stress relief

Correspondences

- Celestial body: Jupiter
- Sign: Libra
- Element: air
- Crystal: howlite
- Herb: valerian root
- Oil: balsam fir

Imagery: A knight or effigy lies in a crypt, and three swords hang above and one lies underneath. The knight has fought his battles bravely and is now being given time to rest before the next battle begins. A stained-glass window above him features the word 'PAX', which means 'peace' in Latin.

Empowering meanings

- This is your permission slip to take time out to retreat, rest and recharge. Modern lives are so busy and there is so much pressure to hustle, keep going and never stop, but a knight cannot fight one battle after another with no rest. This will only result in missed swings and injury or worse.

✦ Take time out before you are knocked out. Understand that rest and recovery are just as important as fighting your battles.

Reversed meanings: A resistance to resting, too much hustle and not enough flow, burning the candle at both ends, burnout. A time of rest being over and getting back to work.

Inquiry questions
✦ How can I bring more rest and relaxation into my life?
✦ Is there anywhere I am resisting rest?

Affirmations
✦ I give myself permission to rest and relax.
✦ I work hard and rest well.

Ritual: Schedule rest into your daily and weekly task lists.

FIVE OF SWORDS

Confrontation, grudges, disloyalty, winning at all costs, communication difficulties, ego, betrayal, bullying, empty victory, unfair fight, no-win situation, hard feelings, wounded pride

Correspondences
- Celestial body: Venus
- Sign: Aquarius
- Element: air
- Crystal: snowflake obsidian
- Herb: sage
- Oil: tarragon

Imagery: A figure in the foreground holds two swords in one hand and one in the other, and two more swords lie by their feet. They seem to have taken everyone else's swords, causing harm and upset to a crying figure near the water. Another figure stands in the centre, unable or choosing not to pick sides.

Empowering meanings
- Check yourself before you wreck yourself.
- Trying to win or succeed at all costs may cause harm or hurt to others in order to satisfy your own ego desires. Don't get so caught up in your goals and dreams that you lose sight of what's really important.
- If you feel betrayed or that someone has taken something from you, the message here is to let go of grudges and

reclaim your power. Learn how to protect your energy and set strong boundaries.

✦ Listen to all sides of a story before taking sides.

Reversed meanings: What's been taken being returned, conflict dying down, things being resolved, grudges let go of, a resolution or arguments settled. A realisation that you need to choose a more aligned way to get what you want.

Inquiry questions
✦ Where am I holding grudges or hard feelings?
✦ How can I see both sides?

Affirmations
✦ I fight for what's right.
✦ I step away from no-win situations.

Ritual: Write down on a piece of paper any grudges or hard feelings you are holding. Burn the paper.

SIX OF SWORDS

Moving on, leaving difficulties behind, smooth sailing, helpers in the spirit realm, supporters, removal of obstacles, patience, safe passage, resolution

Correspondences
- Celestial body: Mercury
- Sign: Aquarius
- Element: air
- Crystal: charoite
- Herb: mugwort
- Oil: palo santo

Imagery: Two figures huddle in blankets in a small boat while six swords stick out in front. They appear to have been through a difficult time and it can be assumed they are travelling with only the clothes on their back. However, they have found safe passage with an oarsman, sometimes representative of a spirit guide or guardian angel, who is guiding them away from the choppy water at the front of the image towards the smooth waters ahead.

Empowering meanings
- Difficulties are now behind you and you are sailing into calmer waters ahead.
- Let others support you and call on the guidance of your spirit guides and angels or loved ones in spirit to help lead you forward.

✦ Trust the journey: better things are ahead of you than what you leave behind.

Reversed meanings: A resistance to moving on, staying where you are even if it's uncomfortable or no longer feels right, a feeling that you've lost your way, being too proud to receive help or guidance.

Inquiry questions
✦ What am I ready to leave behind?
✦ Who can help me move forward?

Affirmations
✦ Better things are coming.
✦ I trust my guides and angels to guide me forward.

Ritual: Visualise that your guardian angel is placing a cloak of peace and love around you to protect you on your journey.

Expanded card meanings

249

SEVEN OF SWORDS

Hidden agenda, strategy, discernment, stealth, taking back what's yours, careful planning, precautions, avoiding confrontation, tact, diplomacy, subterfuge, vigilance, protection

Correspondences
- Celestial bodies: Uranus, moon
- Sign: Aquarius
- Element: air
- Crystal: stichtite
- Herb: hawthorn berry
- Oil: benzoin

Imagery: A figure sneaks away from a camp with five swords in his arms, while two swords stand in the ground. He looks back to make sure no one is following him. Traditionally this is known as a card of deception, a message that someone is stealing from or lying to you, but this figure could just as likely be taking back what was theirs to begin with!

Empowering meanings
- Protect yourself and your interests. This is not a time to blindly trust others or give away your time, energy or money. Be discerning.
- If you have been taking more than you need or keeping things hidden from others it may be time to tell the truth,

make amends and make different, more aligned choices in the future.

✦ Take back your power from those who have taken it from you in the past and from situations that have made you feel less than.

Reversed meanings: Potential to get caught out if you're lying or doing anything dubious. Lies will be uncovered, property returned and justice served.

Inquiry questions
✦ What has been taken from me?
✦ What have I taken from others?

Affirmations
✦ I am discerning in all my affairs.
✦ I take only what I need.

Ritual: Visualise all lost parts of yourself returning like golden puzzle pieces of light and coming back into your aura.

EIGHT OF SWORDS

Trapped, powerless, uncertain, unaware of your own power, hopeless, helpless, lack of self-belief, a problem of your own making, victim mentality, hoping to be rescued, negative cords of attachment, temporary difficulties, limitations, liberation

Correspondences
- Celestial body: Jupiter
- Sign: Gemini
- Element: air
- Crystal: eudialyte
- Herb: motherwort
- Oil: vetiver

Imagery: A figure is bound and blindfolded and surrounded by eight swords sticking into the ground around them. They stand on a puddle of water, suggesting they still have some ability to use their intuition even if it's not very strong. A castle providing possible help stands off in the distance. At first glance the person appears trapped, but their feet are free and could step away from the situation if they would just realise they could do so.

Empowering meanings
- While you may feel trapped or helpless in a situation there is always a way out. Trust yourself, get resourceful and help yourself out of any entanglements you find yourself in.
- No one is coming to save you, but you can save yourself.

- You may be facing a problem of your own making: this is good news! If you made this problem you can also free yourself from it.
- You can get yourself out of this situation, and the best way to do that is to change your mindset around it, believing you can and taking that first step to free yourself.

Reversed meanings: Removal of obstacles, greater clarity, a powerful realisation, freedom and release, taking responsibility for your problems

Inquiry questions
- In what ways am I making problems for myself?
- How can I help myself out of this situation?

Affirmations
- I liberate myself from the ties that bind me.
- I am the hero of my own story.

Ritual: Visualise all negative cords of attachment being cut, cleared and healed.

NINE OF SWORDS

Worry, over-thinking, self-doubt, sleepless nights, anxiety, insomnia, negative thought patterns, guilt, imagining the worst, loneliness, lack of self-compassion, self-fulfilling prophecies

Correspondences

- Celestial body: Mars
- Sign: Gemini
- Element: air
- Crystal: lepidolite
- Herb: chamomile
- Oil: rosemary

Imagery: A figure sits up in bed with their hands over their face as though waking from a nightmare. Nine swords adorn the wall above them, signifying the challenging thoughts they are dealing with. The blanket is covered in red roses, symbolising love, passion and beauty, and astrological signs: a comforting reminder of the enormity of the cosmos's divine guides. Carved into the bed is a figure vanquishing another, a reminder that you can do the same with your own negative thoughts.

Empowering meanings

- Any fear, worry, anxiety, shame or guilt you're experiencing right now is most likely unfounded. You have the power to turn on the light, see there's nothing to be afraid of and release your worry, anxiety and fearful thoughts.

✦ Whatever is keeping you up at night is likely to be imagined, but if it is real it can be faced, solved, changed or accepted. Take power over your mind.

✦ This card can also indicate anxiety or anxiety disorders. If you're struggling to find your way out of fearful thoughts, seek professional support.

Reversed meanings: A time of intense worry is coming to an end, managing anxiety, a realisation that you were worried about nothing, resistance to facing or getting support for your mental health.

Inquiry questions
✦ What am I unnecessarily worrying about?
✦ How can I look after my mental health?

Affirmations
✦ When I face my fears they disappear before me.
✦ I look after my mental health.

Ritual: Sleep with a string of fairy lights or a have night light on to keep bad dreams at bay.

Expanded card meanings

255

TEN OF SWORDS

Completion, end of a difficult cycle, endings, end of a karmic cycle, finality, the last nail in the coffin, the final straw, feeling stabbed in the back, exhaustion, rock bottom, new dawn

Correspondences
- Celestial bodies: Pluto, sun
- Sign: Gemini
- Element: air
- Crystal: prehnite
- Herb: feverfew
- Oil: clary sage

Imagery: A figure lies face down on the sand with 10 swords in their back. They have been completely defeated by whatever or whoever has caused this. This person has been through quite an ordeal, but the struggle is now over and a new day is about to begin.

Empowering meanings
- The struggle is over; this karmic cycle is complete. The challenges and suffering you've been faced with are now or will soon be over.
- All difficult cycles come to a close, and while endings can be difficult to navigate they always signal the beginning of a new cycle, fresh start and different possibilities.

✦ Give yourself time and space to heal, rest and recover from the difficulties of this cycle, then when you're ready step into the start of a bright new chapter.

Reversed meanings: Healing, letting go, moving on, release of suffering and challenges, the start of something new.

Inquiry questions
✦ What has been a struggle?
✦ What cycles are coming to a close?

Affirmations
✦ I let go of the past and look to the future.
✦ A new dawn is rising!

Ritual: Practise deep rest and relaxation. Let things integrate.

PAGE OF SWORDS

Innovative, insightful, logical, studious, new ideas, intellect, learning something new, fresh insights, curiosity, observation, clearing away obstacles

Correspondences

- Celestial body: Mercury
- Signs: Gemini, Libra, Aquarius
- Elements: earth, air
- Crystal: fluorite
- Herb: peppermint
- Oil: tarragon

Imagery: A young page stands on a hill holding a sword high in the air. They appear confident and brave and ready to take on their enemies. Wind sweeps through their hair as clouds and birds surround them, symbolising the clearing element of air.

As a person: A Page of Swords is a young person who is very intelligent and logical, a student or eternal student always with their head in a book, blog or scientific journal. They prefer to make decisions based on facts and are always interested in learning something new.

Their shadow aspects can be that they struggle to express their emotions and do not suffer fools gladly.

Empowering meanings

✦ Clarity is needed. Consider what's blocking you and look at where you may be ignoring hard truths so you can see the path ahead more clearly.

✦ Let go of old stories, negative energy or thinking or anything else that is holding you back so you can start this new chapter on the right foot.

✦ Be open to fresh ideas and points of view.

✦ Clear the air in relationships.

Reversed meanings: Refusing to look at things logically, disconnecting from reality, things feeling uncertain and unclear, refusing to learn or receive new information.

Inquiry questions

✦ What needs to be cut and cleared away?

✦ How can I be more innovative with my challenges or goals?

Affirmations

✦ My energy is clear.

✦ I am ready to start a new, more aligned chapter.

Ritual: Clean and energetically clear your space.

KNIGHT OF SWORDS

Determined, ambitious, driven, overcoming, fast, quick-witted, focused, chivalrous, quick to act, skilful, clever, brave, forceful, clear minded, assertive, communicative

Correspondences

- Celestial body: Mars
- Sign: Gemini
- Element: air
- Crystal: kyanite
- Herb: thyme
- Oil: cypress

Imagery: A knight rides a horse that is galloping at high speed. He is holding on tightly with one hand and holds a sword in the other, focused on his mission and charging forth with great determination.

As a person: A Knight of Swords person is inspiring and exciting to be around, smart and witty and can be quite dashing and charismatic. Life with them is non-stop and can be a lot of fun if you can keep up.

Their shadow aspects can be a lack of control and patience and moving too fast for anyone to keep up with them. They can also be prone to anxiety and find it difficult to rest and relax.

Empowering meanings

✦ No more sitting around: it's time to be assertive and go for what you want! Get focused and determined about your goals and use your drive and ambition to make it happen. Charge forth towards your dreams and purpose.

✦ Speak your truth and communicate your needs and wants clearly.

✦ If things feel as though they are moving too fast for you to keep up right now, this can also be a message to slow your roll.

Reversed meanings: Stuck or stagnant energy, not taking action, going too hard too fast, not being clear on the direction you're travelling in.

Inquiry questions

✦ How can I move swiftly towards my dreams and goals?

✦ What is the danger in going too hard too fast?

Affirmations

✦ I move swiftly towards my goals.

✦ I am on the way!

Ritual: Practise long, slow, deep breathing to keep your energy clear and high.

Expanded card meanings

261

QUEEN OF SWORDS

Intelligent, truthful, reasonable, honest, wise, speaks up for others, defends others, professional, self-reliant, critical minded, fair, just, analytical, stoic, adviser, teacher

Correspondences

- Celestial body: Mercury
- Sign: Libra
- Elements: water, air
- Crystal: celestite
- Herb: dandelion
- Oil: basil

Imagery: The Queen of Swords sits with on a throne on a hill, holding a sword in the air with one hand and the other hand out in front of her as though calling someone forth. She is crowned and wears a robe of clouds. A bird flies overhead and clouds sit in the distance, reminding you that this is a world of intellect and reason.

As a person: A Queen of Swords person is intelligent and wise, knows just about everything and is happy to teach you all they know. They may be a teacher or wise counsel, someone others will go to whenever they need help figuring something out in their lives. Queen of Swords people will always tell you like it is with perhaps a bit of much-needed tough love.

Their shadow aspect is that they can come across as cold, unfeeling or harsh. They may find it difficult to soften their wisdom for those who struggle with cold hard truths.

Empowering meanings

✦ The truth will set you free, so look honestly at the truth of your situation. Consider the ways in which your actions may be sabotaging or blocking you and get real with yourself about the changes you need to make to move forward in a positive way.

✦ Listen to the voices of reason within you and from those you trust.

✦ It may not be comfortable to be confronted with cold, hard truths, but this is often the quickest way through and out of any challenge.

✦ You may be called to take on a role as a teacher, adviser or guide for others.

Reversed meanings: Refusing to acknowledge the truth of a situation, playing the victim, letting others confuse or deceive you, manipulation, disconnection from your heart, not seeing or ignoring reason.

Inquiry questions

✦ How can I be honest with myself?

✦ How can I be a voice of reason for others?

Affirmations

✦ I speak my truth.

✦ The truth will set me free.

Ritual: Journal on your truth and the truth behind any current challenges.

Expanded card meanings

263

KING OF SWORDS

Clear-minded, decisive, rational, sharp and quick, protective, ruthless, objective, intelligent, powerful, self-control, assertive, straightforward, authoritative, uncompromising, integrity

Correspondences
- Celestial body: Saturn
- Sign: Aquarius
- Elements: fire, air
- Crystal: blue chalcedony
- Herb: ginger
- Oil: carrot seed

Imagery: The King of Swords sits confidently on his throne on a hill, a sword in one hand and a serious expression on his face. Clouds drift and birds fly behind him. Butterflies feature on his throne, reminding you of the ability you have to transform your thoughts.

As a person: King of Swords people are logical, analytical and intellectual. They focus on facts and figures when making decisions and can also help others see their choices more clearly. Mind-over-matter people, they have strong integrity and morals and always aim to do what's right.

In their shadow aspect they can be overly critical of themselves or others, have very high exceptions of themselves and others and can struggle to see things from a different perspective. They have a strong desire to always be right and may be prone to anxiety.

Empowering meanings
- Look at your situation logically. Analyse the pros and cons, weigh things up and make sure you have scrutinised all the information before moving forward.
- Develop mastery over your mind. Meditate and work on releasing and rewriting negative thought patterns. Use the power of your mind to create new pathways.
- Move forward with integrity and everything else will fall into place.

Reversed meanings: Being overly critical or too analytical. Ignoring logic and reason, getting out of integrity, questionable moral decisions, struggling with your mindset, letting negative thoughts take over.

Inquiry questions
- What is the logical thing to do here?
- Is my current mindset hindering or helping?

Affirmations
- I am the master of my mind.
- I have strong integrity.

Ritual: Close your eyes and meditate on your breath. Let your thoughts come and go. Calm your mind.

ACE OF PENTACLES

Investment, material gain, opportunities, seeds planted, prosperity, new career or work, new positive financial situation, new projects, resources, stability, abundance

Correspondences
- Celestial body: Earth
- Sign: Capricorn
- Element: earth
- Crystal: magnetite
- Herb: alfalfa
- Oil: clove

Imagery: A disembodied hand appears again out of a cloud, this time holding a large golden pentacle. The pentacle is a symbol of the material world and the element of earth. Beneath the hand is an abundant garden, showing you what's possible when seeds are planted, nourished and nurtured and able to achieve full growth.

Empowering meanings
- Whatever you want to grow in your garden of abundance must first be planted by you. Sow seeds now so that you can harvest rewards in the future.
- Be open to abundance, prosperity, money and work or business opportunities. A small project or offer may turn into something much bigger than expected.
- Be grateful for the little things and more will grow.

Reversed meanings: An inability to hold on to money, spending more than you're earning, unconscious spending, too much focus on money and material things.

Inquiry questions

✦ How can I plant seeds for a more abundant financial future?

✦ How can I be open to receiving more material wealth?

Affirmations

✦ I am abundant.

✦ My prosperity is growing every day.

Ritual: Draw a pentacle with a pen, oil or light on your credit/debit cards. Open your online banking app and draw a pentacle of light over the screen.

Expanded card meanings

TWO OF PENTACLES

Multitasking, flexibility, priorities, responsibilities, balance, juggling, balanced finances, lots on your plate, balance between work and play, adaptability, play, the dance of life, flow of abundance

Correspondences

- Celestial body: Jupiter
- Sign: Capricorn
- Element: earth
- Crystal: scolecite
- Herb: gotu kola
- Oil: fennel

Imagery: A figure balances or juggles two pentacles that are held within a lemniscate (infinity symbol), an emblem of the flow of abundance. Behind them is a stormy sea with two ships also trying to keep their balance. In spite of the storm the figure and boats are able to keep things balanced. Although there seems to be some challenge here, there is also lightness as the figure dances to keep the pentacles in the air.

Empowering meanings

- Bring things into balance. Balance your finances, making sure bills have been paid, and know where your money is going.
- Get into the flow of abundance. Don't hoard your wealth or spend beyond your means, but let money come in and out with ease.

- If you feel that you have too much on your plate, this is a reminder to balance work and play. Find some lightness and playfulness in life.

Reversed meanings: Dropping the ball, a need for more sustainable ways of getting things done, resistance towards sorting out finances, resistance to play, joy or balance.

Inquiry questions
- What needs my attention and focus?
- How can I find more balance between work and play?

Affirmations
- My finances are balanced.
- I dance and flow with life.

Ritual: Dance party! Draw and visualise infinity symbols all around you as you flow and dance with the music.

Three of Pentacles

Collaboration, critique, group work, creation, study, apprenticeship, art, skill, master of your craft, recognition, mentoring, renovation, evaluation, aesthetics

Correspondences
- Celestial body: Mars
- Sign: Capricorn
- Element: earth
- Crystal: amazonite
- Herb: chicory
- Oil: chamomile

Imagery: Three figures work together under an ornate archway, a symbol of a portal or initiation. A craftsperson stands on a bench while the others look on with a diagram, advising and checking the work.

Empowering meanings
- Work with others to achieve your goals. Whether it's moving forward in your career, a creative project or a big dream you are working on manifesting, ask for support and let others help you. You may be called to help someone else on their path.
- Use criticism as an opportunity to learn and grow. Learn from those who are more experienced than you. A mentor or coach can help you get to the next level.

✦ Working with others can be an initiation or challenge for you to overcome and grow through, but collaboration is often essential to manifest your dreams and move forward.

Reversed meanings: Challenging collaborative situations, someone not pulling their weight in group-work situations, trying to do everything yourself, resistance to asking for or accepting help, inability to accept feedback or positive criticism.

Inquiry questions
✦ How could collaboration help me make my dreams come true?
✦ How can I accept positive criticism and feedback with grace?

Affirmations
✦ I always receive the help I need.
✦ I am open to learning from others.

Ritual: Draw a mind map, vision board or blueprint for something you'd like to create or achieve.

FOUR OF PENTACLES

Protection, frugality, holding on, possessiveness, holding or hoarding wealth, love of money, security, protecting what you've worked for, savings, boundaries

Correspondences
- Celestial body: sun
- Sign: Capricorn
- Element: earth
- Crystal: nuummite
- Herb: catnip
- Oil: blue yarrow

Imagery: A crowned figure sits on a chair high above a city. One pentacle sits above his crown, while another is held in his arms and two are under his feet. Often considered to symbolise a miser, greed or control of wealth, this imagery can also suggest someone who is holding tightly on to their resources or protecting what they have worked for.

Empowering meanings
- Protect and hold on tightly to what you have worked so hard for.
- Others may be trying to take more from you – money or other resources, including your energy and time – than you have to give. If this is the case, hold on tightly to what's yours and set strong, healthy boundaries with others.

- If you are hoarding money or any other resources you may block the flow of abundance.

- Practise non-attachment to your desires and outcomes to find more peace, joy and happiness in the here and now.

- Consider where you need to protect what's yours and where to share more of what you have so you can create more blessings in the lives of others.

Reversed meanings: Letting go of your grip, releasing attachment, sharing wealth, blessing others, flow of abundance, potentially giving too much of yourself.

Inquiry questions
- Where am I holding on too tightly?
- How can I experience the flow of abundance?

Affirmations
- I release my grip and move into flow.
- I am a portal for blessings.

Ritual: Take four coins and hold each one separately in your hand, thinking of something you want to release as you do so. Put the coins in a charity container next time you see one.

FIVE OF PENTACLES

Struggle, lack, insecurity, uncertainty, limiting beliefs, worry, a need to ask for help, helping yourself, feeling out in the cold, unexpected expenses

Correspondences

- Celestial body: Mercury
- Sign: Taurus
- Element: earth
- Crystal: petrified wood
- Herb: linden
- Oil: ho-wood

Imagery: Two figures who look to be experiencing some financial hardship and ill-health are walking through the snow. Behind them is a church with a big, bright, stained-glass window, suggesting that help is available to them if they can take a step to help themselves.

Empowering meanings

- If limiting beliefs, worry and insecurity are plaguing you right now, try not to fret. You have options. Help yourself by reframing negative thoughts and beliefs that may be keeping you stuck.
- Ask others for the help and support you need. You do not have to do this on your own; there are plenty of people out there willing and wanting to help you through this.

Reversed meanings: Moving out of a lack of consciousness, asking for help, helping yourself, getting the help you need, being too proud to change the situation

Inquiry questions
✦ Where do I need to help myself?

✦ Do I resist asking for help, and why or why not?

Affirmations
✦ I can help myself out of and through any difficult situation.

✦ People are happy to help me.

Ritual: Ask your guides, angels or the universe for what you need.

Expanded card meanings

SIX OF PENTACLES

Giving, receiving, charity, equity, generosity, accepting help, goodness of heart, sharing the wealth, kindness, support, prosperity, energy exchange

Correspondences
- Celestial bodies: moon, Venus
- Sign: Taurus
- Element: earth
- Crystal: moss agate
- Herb: flaxseed
- Oil: bergamot

Imagery: A wealthy man dressed in a bright red robe stands above two figures who appear less well off. In one hand the man holds a set of balanced scales to symbolise equity and balance, and in the other he holds gold coins that pour into the hands of a figure below him in a symbol of generosity and good-heartedness.

Empowering meanings
- Be generous and do some good with the resources you have: money, time, energy, knowledge and wisdom. Share what you have with others with an open heart.
- If you're on the other end of the scale right now, open yourself up to receiving from others. Don't be too proud to take a handout, and let people help and support you when

you need it. The scales will tip again, and you will have more to give to others again in future.

✦ Support charities or organisations that are close to your heart.

Reversed meanings: Energy, time or money not being spent wisely, imbalanced energy exchange, not enough give and take, inability to receive, being too proud to receive from others.

Inquiry questions
✦ How can I share my wealth in ways that make a positive difference?
✦ What can I be open to receiving?

Affirmations
✦ I give with an open heart.
✦ I gratefully receive the blessings offered to me.

Ritual: Give to charity in whatever way you are able.

SEVEN OF PENTACLES

Reflection, evaluation, patience, assessing progress, perseverance, long-term planning, waiting, slow and steady progress, unfulfilled, discontent, tiredness, lack of job satisfaction, procrastination

Correspondences
- Celestial body: Saturn
- Sign: Taurus
- Element: earth
- Crystal: ametrine
- Herb: oregano
- Oil: mint

Imagery: A worker who's been tending the fields pauses, leaning on his rake to assess what has grown and is now ready for harvest. He appears tired and a little dissatisfied about his crop, even though it's very abundant.

Empowering meanings
- Reflect on and assess the current situation, looking at what has grown, what goals have been reached and what has yet to grow.
- It may be time to seek something more fulfilling: a new job or career path may be calling. If you can't change the situation look for ways to find more fulfilment in other areas of your life.
- Patience may be needed. If you can stick things out a little longer you may see bigger rewards in the long term.

Reversed meanings: Impatience, giving up too quickly, not seeing something to fruition, valuing small, short-term gains over long-term ones, staying in an unfulfilling situation, resistance to working for others.

Inquiry questions
✦ Where am I feeling unfulfilled?
✦ Where do I need to have more patience?

Affirmations
✦ I give things time to grow.
✦ My abundance is growing.

Ritual: Write a list of things that fulfil you and do one of them each day.

EIGHT OF PENTACLES

Hard work, dedication, skill, talent, focus, satisfaction, creativity, good work ethic, art, craft, studious, job satisfaction, hard work paying off, effort, diligence, perfectionism

Correspondences
- Celestial body: sun
- Sign: Virgo
- Element: earth
- Crystal: topaz
- Herb: rowan
- Oil: pine

Imagery: A craftsperson sits on a bench hard at work making a pentacle. Six pentacles hang on the tree above and one lies at their feet, showing you this craftsperson has been dedicated to honing their craft.

Empowering meanings
- Stay focused on the task at hand and what you're trying to achieve. Finish what you've started. Do a good job that you can be satisfied and proud of.
- If you want to get better at something, from creative pursuits and career skills to communication and relationships, work on putting what you've learned into practice.
- You have many skills and talents and your goals are within reach!

✦ This card can also suggest a need to work on yourself.

Reversed meanings: Lack of job satisfaction, hard work doesn't feel like it's paying off, work of poor quality, unfinished projects.

Inquiry questions
✦ What do I want to get better at or master?
✦ What kind of work, hobbies or activities light me up?

Affirmations
✦ My hard work pays off.
✦ I am a master of my craft.

Ritual: Draw eight pentacles and write the above affirmations underneath. Place this image next to your desk or wherever you work.

NINE OF PENTACLES

Self-sufficiency, prosperity, luxury, success, attainment, accomplishment, fulfilment, elegance, independence, rewards for hard work, abundance, self-employment, enjoying your own company

Correspondences

- Celestial body: Venus
- Sign: Virgo
- Element: earth
- Crystal: jade
- Herb: strawberry
- Oil: bay leaf

Imagery: A well-off woman stands in an abundant garden of nine pentacles with a falcon, a symbol of mastery, freedom and independence, calmly perched on her hand. Off in the distance can be seen this woman's large house or castle.

Empowering meanings

- Enjoy the fruits of your labour. If the abundance isn't yet here, keep working hard for the life you want and trust that it is coming.
- Make sensible financial decisions. Consider the future when it comes to your spending.
- There is positive energy here if you own a business or want to feel more financially independent, especially as a woman.

✦ Enjoy and work on your independence in any area of your life. You can do amazing things all on your own!

Reversed meanings: An inability to hold abundance, difficulties with saving money, relying too much on others for your financial needs, resistance to or difficulties in successful self-employment.

Inquiry questions
✦ How can I be more self-sufficient?
✦ How can I look after the abundance and prosperity I already have?

Affirmations
✦ I am wealthy and abundant.
✦ I am financially independent.

Ritual: Bless nine coins or crystals with the energy of infinite prosperity. Keep them in your purse or home to remind you of your abundance.

Expanded card meanings

TEN OF PENTACLES

Community, legacy, wealth, inheritance, prosperity, financial success, ancestors, ancestral healing, home, family, generations, financial security, providing for others, family pets

Correspondences
- Celestial body: Mercury
- Sign: Virgo
- Element: earth
- Crystal: fairy stone
- Herb: blackberry
- Oil: bergamot

Imagery: Three generations, including the family dogs, gather in the courtyard of a large estate. This is an abundant and happy scene of generational wealth, community connection and security.

Empowering meanings
- Share the wealth. Gift your money, time, wisdom and knowledge so it benefits all.
- Be open to receiving help and support from your elders and those who've achieved what you are trying to do.
- Connect with your community. Offer what you can and receive what you need from others.

✦ Create a legacy through your family line, creative work or simply in the way you touch the hearts and lives of others in positive ways.

Reversed meanings: Resistance to sharing your wealth or wisdom, disconnected from community, isolation, guilt or shame about your financial situation, a need for ancestral healing.

Inquiry questions
✦ What legacy am I creating?
✦ How can those who've come before me guide and support me?

Affirmations
✦ I am wealthy, wise and abundant.
✦ When I share my wealth I feel even more abundant.

Ritual: Visualise green healing light moving through and healing prosperity patterns in your ancestral line.

PAGE OF PENTACLES

Studious, practical, grounded, focused, ambitious, diligent, conscientious, scholarly, steady, planning for the future

Correspondences

- Celestial body: Earth
- Signs: Taurus, Virgo, Capricorn
- Element: earth
- Crystal: bronzite
- Herb: cowslip
- Oil: nutmeg

Imagery: A young page stands confidently in a meadow of flowers that are beginning to grow, a symbol of new beginnings. The page looks intently at the pentacle in their hands, showing you that material needs are their focus.

As a person: A Page of Pentacles is a young person who is grounded, practical and goal oriented and focused on creating a positive and abundant future for themselves. Page of Pentacles people are students of the material who want to learn all they can about money and finances and/or the natural world.

Their shadow aspects include being so focused on material success they lose sight of or no longer make time for other aspects of their life, including friends, family, their health and well-being or their spiritual path.

Empowering meanings

✦ Plan for your abundance and prosperity. Think ahead rather than focusing on instant gratification. Do things that your future self would thank you for. It's never too late to plan for the future.

✦ Learn more about financial systems, studying or training for a new, better-paying career, or learn more about the natural world around you.

✦ Ground your energy. Spend time in nature, eat well, stay well rested and look after your physical well-being.

Reversed meanings: Not planning for the future, overspending, staying in the dark about your own finances, being ungrounded.

Inquiry questions

✦ How can I plan for the future?

✦ What do I need to learn that would help me build more wealth?

Affirmations

✦ I am abundant and ambitious.

✦ I can achieve all of my financial goals.

Ritual: Place a small flower and a coin on your altar as a symbol of your growing abundance.

Expanded card meanings

KNIGHT OF PENTACLES

Goal-oriented, consistent, diligent, hard-working, stable, strong, ambitious, reliable, upholding standards, responsible, patient, dependable, predictable

Correspondences
- Celestial body: Mercury
- Sign: Virgo
- Elements: air, earth
- Crystal: green Jasper
- Herb: balmony
- Oil: lavender

Imagery: A knight on a horse holds a pentagram out in front of them. The landscape looks flat, and although this knight appears to be on a journey the horse is standing still, suggesting slow but steady movement.

As a person: A Knight of Pentacles person takes their time and gets things right. They do not rush or worry, but trust and know they will arrive at their destination in perfect divine timing. Steady, stable and strong, they are focused on long-term success and building their dreams and empires one brick at a time.

Their shadow aspects are that they can become stubborn and get so stuck in their ways they stop moving completely. They may become lazy or lose interest in their work, goals or dreams.

Empowering meanings

✦ Slow and steady wins the race: you will get where you are going eventually, so just relax and enjoy the journey. Take breaks as you work on moving towards your goals and manifesting your dreams. Enjoy the scenery, be grateful and be here now. Instead of focusing on the destination, try to enjoy and be present for each step of the way.

✦ Make regular small steps forward and you will get where you want to go!

Reversed meanings: Getting stuck, not moving at all, not taking action, laziness, focus on instant gratification, resistance to the present, always wanting to be at the destination already.

Inquiry questions

✦ What is taking longer than I would like it to?

✦ What is my next step?

Affirmations

✦ I have time.

✦ I trust the journey.

Ritual: Draw a pentagram and write your goals and destinations around it. Place it on your altar or somewhere you'll see it often.

Expanded card meanings

289

QUEEN OF PENTACLES

Abundant, generous, comfortable, dependable, successful, wealthy, nurturing, luxury, gratitude, encouragement, love of nature, motherly, kind-hearted, down to earth, steadfast, body wisdom

Correspondences

- Celestial body: Venus
- Sign: Capricorn
- Elements: water, earth
- Crystal: emerald
- Herb: echinacea
- Oil: jasmine

Imagery: A queen sits on her throne surrounded by an abundance of plants and red roses, symbols of love and the divine feminine. She gently holds a pentacle on her lap and looks at it with love and gratitude. The image exudes warmth, cosiness and comfort.

As a person: Queen of Pentacles people are warm and generous with their wealth, love, time and energy and are grounded and patient. They have learned so much on their journey of creating a beautiful life for themselves and they love sharing their wisdom and wealth with others. They are grateful for all they have and enjoy nurturing and teaching others to be successful and prosperous in their own lives.

Their shadow aspects can be that they either hoard their wealth or are so generous they have nothing left for themselves.

They may also struggle with intimacy and prefer to show their love through gifts or money.

Empowering meanings
✦ Be grateful for all you've created, manifested and received. Count your blessings, of which there are so many! Continue to nurture and encourage the seeds you have planted to keep growing into even more abundance. Share your wealth, time, experience and heart with others.

✦ Remember that true wealth and success are not found in numbers in your bank account, but in abundance in all its forms: love, friendship, family, health, happiness, opportunities, time and so on.

✦ Nurture yourself and all you want to see grow in your life.

Reversed meanings: Building wealth at the cost of losing what's important, expecting money to be the answer to your problems, unwise spending, not sharing the wealth, blocked prosperity flow.

Inquiry questions
✦ What is my definition of success?
✦ How can I create a beautiful life for myself?

Affirmations
✦ I am abundant, successful and happy.
✦ I nurture my dreams and trust in their growth.

Ritual: Treat yourself with one of life's little luxuries.

KING OF PENTACLES

Steadfast, wealthy, stable, reliable, responsible, grounded, secure, provider, practical, protective, wise, hard-working, financial security, prosperity consciousness, mastery of the material realm

Correspondences

- Celestial body: Saturn
- Sign: Taurus
- Elements: fire, earth
- Crystal: garnet
- Herb: mandrake
- Oil: patchouli

Imagery: A king sits on a throne with his head high. He holds a pentacle in one hand and a sceptre in the other. His throne is adorned by the bull, a symbol of earth, and his castle sits in the background, showing you that this is a man who has amassed great wealth.

As a person: King of Pentacles people are wealthy and successful, or working towards it, and grounded and stable. They make great leaders, teachers, advisors and providers.

Their shadow aspects can include being overly focused on career and finances or emotionally unavailable. They may also lose sight of what true wealth really is.

Empowering meanings

✦ Own your success and abundance. Be proud of yourself and all that you've achieved.

✦ Use your wealth and experience to help others.

✦ Provide for and protect others, whether that's through financial support or by offering advice, support, guidance and your time or contacts.

✦ Be a strong, stable, generous and grounded influence on all those around you, but most of all be that for yourself too!

✦ Continue to work hard towards your goals and create even more wealth and goodness for yourself, family and community.

Reversed meanings: Challenges with finances, having money but spending it all, struggle to create abundance, thinking you won't be happy until you have more, being jealous of people who have more than you.

Inquiry questions

✦ How can I embody my success?

✦ How can I share the wealth?

Affirmations

✦ I am rich, healthy and happy.

✦ I am abundant in all ways!

Ritual: Look at your finances with your third eye open and make smart financial decisions.

Expanded card meanings

TROUBLESHOOTING GUIDE

Here's a quick guide to troubleshooting your readings.

YOUR READING FEELS SCARY

+ Revisit the scary cards section on pages 43 to 47.
+ Read the empowered messages in the expanded card meanings chapter.
+ Pull a clarifying card for more information about what the card means in this context.
+ If a scary card has fallen in the position of a potential outcome, remember that it's only ever a potential. You have the power to change the course of your destiny. The cards do not create your fate; you do!
+ Talk to someone you trust and who reads tarot in an empowered way. You can always reach out to me via my website or social media accounts: I am always happy to help reframe a scary reading into an empowering and positive one!

YOUR READING DOESN'T MAKE SENSE

+ Be sure to prepare your energy and know who you're communicating with through the cards before you begin.
+ Make sure you are asking clear questions.

- ✦ Try to avoid reading the cards when you're in extreme emotional states. You can still read during emotionally difficult times – in fact, this is when you may most need the tarot – but when you're very angry or feel deep grief, for example, you may not be in the right frame of mind to see your readings with clarity and hope.
- ✦ Don't rush your readings: take your time to slowly go through each card.
- ✦ Avoid pulling more and more cards to try to make sense of things as this can add more information and thus confusion.
- ✦ Trust your intuition: sometimes readings get unclear and confused when you start second-guessing your guidance. That first thing you thought or felt when you turned over the card is usually the right message.

- When looking at the expanded card meanings chapter only take what resonates. There may be just one keyword or one small sentence in that section that feels right for your reading, so take that and leave the rest.
- If you're really struggling with just one particular card, pull another card to clarify the message.
- Consider whether the reading is unclear or you're just not getting the messages you wanted. Doing some shadow work can help with this.
- You may be doing too many readings, which can create a kind of psychic burnout. Pace yourself.
- Avoid asking the same question over and over again without taking action on the guidance you've received.
- If you're finding reading with reversals challenging, only read with upright cards.
- Clear your deck, reset your energy and try again.
- Remember that for most people it takes time and practice to be able to read the cards clearly and confidently every time. Keep practising and working through the murky readings and you will find all the answers you are seeking!

ABOUT THE AUTHOR

Victoria 'Vix' Maxwell is the creator of New Age Hipster, a spiritual home for good witches, lightworkers, star seeds and spiritual seekers. A priestess for the present time, modern mystic and spiritual teacher in Converse sneakers, she supports her worldwide community with reconnecting to their own light, inner guidance and power through the Light Club spiritual development membership, soul readings and spiritual healings, Akashic records rewrites, kundalini yoga classes, spiritual business and author mentoring, podcasts and award-winning blog and social media channels.

Vix is the author of the bestselling young adult fiction series *Santolsa Saga* and of *Witch, Please: Empowerment and enlightenment for the modern mystic*, *Manifest Your Dreams* and the *Angels Among Us, Goddesses Among Us* and *Galactic Guides* oracle decks, as well as the *Oracle Card Companion*.

newagehipster.co | **f** 🅾 ♪ **newagehipster333**

300   TAROT CARD COMPANION